The
Perfect
Mix

The
Perfect
Mix

Bread, Soup, Dessert,
and Other Homemade Mixes
from Your Kitchen

Diane Phillips

HEARST BOOKS
NEW YORK

To Eleanore, Bill, David, and Paul.
Thank you for allowing me to be
a part of your lives.

Library of Congress Cataloging-in-Publication Data

Phillips, Diane.
    The perfect mix : bread, soup, dessert, and other homemade mixes from your kitchen / Diane Phillips.
        p.   cm.
    Includes index.
    ISBN 0-688-12104-7
    1. Food mixes.   I. Title.
    TX652.P47   1993
    641.5′5—dc20   92-41328
                                                                         CIP

Printed in the United States of America

First Edition

            6   7   8   9   10

BOOK DESIGN BY LIZ TROVATO

Acknowledgments

W hile writing this book I have been privileged to work with people who have given me the benefit of their knowledge, support, and encouragement.

I would first like to thank my agent, Susan Travis at the McBride Agency, for her friendship and confidence. A special thank you to Margret McBride and Winifred Golden for their help as well.

No one could ever have received more support and guidance from an editor than I have received from Harriet Bell. I see her as the conductor of the symphony, bringing together the different sounds to create the music. Her enthusiasm for this book is contagious, and I feel fortunate to have had this opportunity to work with such a gifted editor. Thank you also to Robbie Capp for her exceptional job at copyediting. I would also like to express my appreciation to Liz Trovato for designing the book, as well as to Susan Goldman for the beautiful cover photograph. And thank you to Valerie Cimino for always having an answer when I needed one.

I am indebted to the many friends and family members who have blessed me with their love. In particular, I would like to thank my children, Carrie and Ryan. Their patience and understanding as well as their enthusiastic support as tasters are appreciated. My husband, Chuck, who has been my best friend for twenty-four years, deserves a special thank you and hug for always being there.

Contents

Introduction

T he gifts I have always treasured the most have been homemade and handmade. Whether a popsicle-stick picture frame made by one of my children or a quilt made by a friend, these gifts say, "Thank you, you are special and I appreciate you."

When my children were small, I began giving my neighbors gifts from my kitchen at Christmas. I baked four or five different types of cookies and put them into decorative reusable tins. My interest in giving gifts from my kitchen took a new turn one day when I was shopping in a gift store and saw a package of beer-bread mix. When I read the ingredients on the label, I realized that this was the same bread I had been baking for years. Rather than pay a high price for a mix I could easily put together at home, I came up with the idea of making my own, packing it in a whimsical, yet useful, container with a detailed recipe card attached. The next year I made bread mixes and gave them to friends as well as to those who made my life easier: the mailman, teachers, and the staff at the doctor's office.

By finding unique containers for each of the mixes, I have been able to create unusual gifts from my kitchen. One advantage to these gifts is that, for the most part, they are not perishable, so they do not have to be used immediately. From bread mixes, I moved on to desserts, dips, soups, and rice mixes, and each one serves as a delicious reminder of the gift giver.

The mixes in this book make lovely gifts all by themselves, but can also be mixed and matched to create a larger theme basket, or can be given with items that will tie the theme together. For example, give coffee and cake mixes together with dessert plates, cups, and saucers— china if a formal gift is appropriate, pretty paper goods if a more casual gift is called for.

Too often, we feel so rushed that we don't have the energy to think about making gifts for others. The idea conjures up images of month-long projects or seemingly endless hours of labor for very small results. Or, if you're like me, you quake at the notion of doing anything remotely "crafty." I usually succeed in glue-gunning myself to most projects. But the gift mixes in this book require very little time to put together and many of them can be doubled or tripled to save time.

Gift giving at my house is a year-round event, whether to say thank you to a hostess or as a token of appreciation for a special teacher. I have given each of these recipes over the years, and I enjoy the giving as much as my friends have enjoyed the receiving.

Supplies

Containers

Finding containers for your gifts is almost as much fun as making the gifts to go in them. Baskets are an obvious choice, as well as small jars and bowls. Import and other gift shops carry wide ranges of glass, wicker, and pottery that can be used as containers. Some greeting card companies sell tins, bags, and cardboard containers for cookies and confections. Painted wooden boxes are available during the Christmas holidays for gift giving. One of my favorite containers is from Eucalyptus Stoneware (see Source Guide), ceramic baskets made in Del Mar, California, near my home. These baskets can even go into the oven for warming bread and rolls.

For rice mixes, use a large lotus bowl with four smaller ones as gift containers. You might like to give the rice mix in an ovenproof casserole or layer the mix in a clear jar. Soup mixes packaged in cellophane bags can be put inside a soup tureen.

Spices can be given in any airtight jar that can be labeled. Some stores that carry housewares sell spice jars and airtight jars with rubber seals. You can also recycle empty spice bottles to refill with herb and spice mixes. Wash the bottles in hot soapy water and remove labels. Fill the jars with the spice blend, tie bows around the jar tops, and attach a recipe to each.

Bread and dessert mixes should also be packed in airtight containers. Florist's cellophane bags, used to wrap corsages, come in a variety of sizes. Plastic bags that have been sealed airtight, and glass and ceramic jars or canisters are also suitable for these mixes. Cellophane makes a more beautiful presentation, but cling plastic is perfectly acceptable. Decorate bags with seasonal stickers: At Christmastime, use Santa Claus or reindeer stickers, and pumpkin stickers for Halloween. Baggies or similar plastic wraps can also be used, tied with ribbon. Decorate white paper lunch bags with stickers or stamped designs. Fold the top of the bag over about two and a half inches. With a hole punch, make two holes near the top, about two and a half inches apart, and string ribbon through, then attach a gift card to the ribbon.

Beverage mixes can be presented in coffeepots, teapots, pitchers, canisters, and thermoses, as well as in seasonal or occasion-related coffee mugs, which can be filled with mix and sealed with cling plastic wraps.

When traveling, I try to find interesting containers to transform into great gifts when I return home. Antiques stores and yard sales are excellent places to discover unique crystal, porcelain ware, and antique jars for gift giving.

Wrapping Supplies

Paper products for wrapping gifts can be found at stationery stores and greeting card shops. Florist's cellophane bags can be bought at florist supply stores, or perhaps at your local florist. Clear and colored cellophane wrap is available at greeting card stores, or look in the Yellow Pages under florist, supply or florist, wholesale. Most paper-goods stores sell plastic bags with zip-top closures, from the one-tablespoon size to three-quart size. Small zip-type bags are especially good for spice mixes that accompany a soup mix. Inexpensive ribbons in a myriad of colors can be purchased in large quantities from wholesale florist suppliers as well as at craft shops, stationery and chain variety stores.

When shopping for linens to line the baskets that hold my mix containers, I have found that discount department stores have a great selection of napkins and other linens. These stores also carry lovely porcelain ware.

For gift tag instructions, carefully print or type them on a sheet of white paper. Ask your local photocopy store to reduce your instructions in size, so that four copies fit onto a standard 8½- by 11-inch sheet of paper. Your master sheet then contains four copies of the recipe. Select a color of card stock (heavy paper), and have the recipes reproduced on it. By printing four per sheet, you save money. Have the store cut the cards for you. Once you're ready to use them, punch a hole in the upper-left corner to string ribbon through.

Herbs and Spices

When making gifts, you may want to buy your supplies in large quantities. Warehouse stores, restaurant-supply companies, and health-food stores often carry bulk spices and supplies. Buying in quantity can help to cut the expense of your gift giving. Several friends can split the cost of ingredients or wrapping materials to cut costs further. Making gifts with friends is one of my favorite ways to spend a day or evening.

Dressing, Dip, and Seasoning Mixes

Given a choice, I would select fresh herbs over dry. But, when fresh herbs are unavailable, a combination of dried herbs brings out the flavors of a dish. The herbs and spices in this chapter are combined to create a variety of dressings, dips, and seasoning blends. Whole peppercorns in a rainbow of colors are blended together for the elegant Pepper Mill Combo Mix (see page 12) to show off in a Lucite pepper mill. Herbes de Provence Mix (see page 16), Cajun Seasoning Mix (see page 20), and Artichoke Spice Mix (see page 22) will all be welcome additions to a friend's spice shelf, and dip and dressing mixes become creative tools to enhance an everyday meal.

The mixes in this chapter are made with dried herbs and spices that will keep for months. Whenever possible, buy whole spices rather than crushed, ground, or rubbed ones. When whole spices are crushed, oils are released, and the spices lose their potency. If you prefer to use fresh garlic or lemon peel, add them to the basket and amend the directions.

Containers for herbs and spices should be airtight. Cellophane and small zip-type plastic bags can be used for these mixes. Many housewares stores sell glass and earthenware jars, with a variety of airtight lids. And remember to recycle empty spice jars. Tie a ribbon around the top of the jar or use pinking shears and cut circles of fabric twice the diameter of the jar top, cover with the fabric, and secure in place with a ribbon tied around the jar neck.

Other good holders for seasoning mixes are those big salt and pepper shakers and sugar containers they have at lunch counters (which you can buy at restaurant supply houses). The insides of their lids can be lined with cling plastic wraps or foil to seal the shaker holes.

Ranch-style
Dressing and Dip Mix

Makes ¼ cup

T his versatile mix can be used to make a dressing for salads, a dip for fresh vegetables, or topping for baked potatoes or steamed vegetables. Pack the mixture into a small spice jar or cellophane bag. Place it in a wooden salad bowl with salad servers and a dressing cruet, then wrap the bowl in colored cellophane.

1½ tablespoons dried
  parsley
1 tablespoon salt
½ tablespoon dried chives
¼ tablespoon dried
  oregano

¼ tablespoon dried
  tarragon
½ tablespoon garlic
  powder
½ tablespoon lemon
  pepper

In a medium bowl, combine all the ingredients. Store in an airtight container.

Ranch Dressing
Makes 1 cup

½ cup mayonnaise
½ cup buttermilk

1 tablespoon Ranch-
style Dressing and
Dip Mix

In a large bowl, whisk together the mayonnaise, butter-milk, and dressing and dip mix. Refrigerate for one hour before serving.

Ranch Dip
Makes 2 cups

2 tablespoons Ranch-
style Dressing and
Dip Mix
1 cup mayonnaise or
low-fat mayonnaise

1 cup sour cream or
low-fat yogurt

Combine the Ranch-style Dressing and Dip Mix with mayonnaise and sour cream. Refrigerate for 2 hours before serving with raw vegetables, or as a topping for baked potatoes or steamed vegetables.

Dillweed Dip Mix

Makes 1¾ cups

T his dip mix is so versatile, it has become one of my favorites for giving. What a charming hostess gift, packed into a spice jar topped with a bow, or a little cellophane bag tied with ribbon. Set the jar or bag into a small dip bowl, such as a tempura-sauce dish, and rest the bowl on a tempura plate to be used as a vegetable and dip set. Wrap plate and bowl in cellophane and you have a terrific housewarming gift.

½ cup dried dillweed
½ cup dried minced
   onion
½ cup dried parsley

⅓ cup Spice Islands Beau
   Monde seasoning

In a small glass bowl, combine all the ingredients and place in a container.

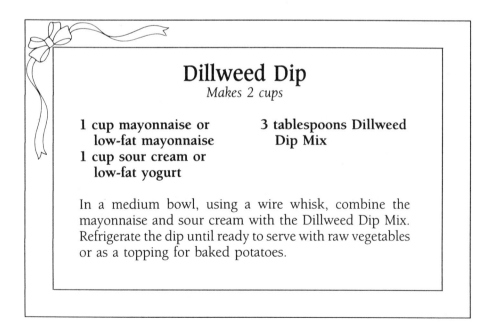

Dillweed Dip
Makes 2 cups

1 cup mayonnaise or
   low-fat mayonnaise
1 cup sour cream or
   low-fat yogurt

3 tablespoons Dillweed
   Dip Mix

In a medium bowl, using a wire whisk, combine the mayonnaise and sour cream with the Dillweed Dip Mix. Refrigerate the dip until ready to serve with raw vegetables or as a topping for baked potatoes.

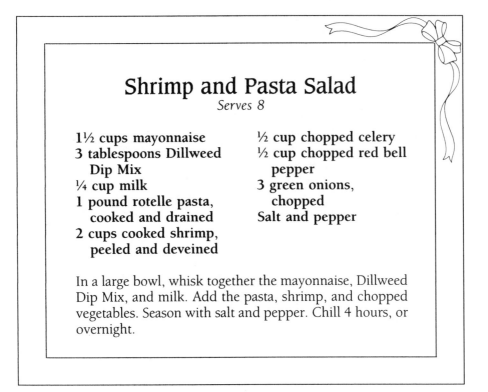

Shrimp and Pasta Salad
Serves 8

1½ cups mayonnaise
3 tablespoons Dillweed
  Dip Mix
¼ cup milk
1 pound rotelle pasta,
  cooked and drained
2 cups cooked shrimp,
  peeled and deveined

½ cup chopped celery
½ cup chopped red bell
  pepper
3 green onions,
  chopped
Salt and pepper

In a large bowl, whisk together the mayonnaise, Dillweed Dip Mix, and milk. Add the pasta, shrimp, and chopped vegetables. Season with salt and pepper. Chill 4 hours, or overnight.

Mexican Fiesta
Dip Mix

Makes 7 ¼-cup packages

T his is an unusual Southwestern dip mix that can be given in a
small sombrero. The crown of the sombrero can be indented to
hold a dip bowl, and the brim can be lined with napkins to accommo-
date tortilla chips. If you have trouble finding one, there is a ceramic
sombrero available through Crate and Barrel (see Source Guide), or try
a party supply store. Another idea for a party gift is to pack this mix
into a small spice jar, and include it in a basket with a terra-cotta dip
bowl, blue corn tortilla chips, four margarita glasses, a bottle of tequila,
Triple Sec, coarse salt, and some limes.

½ cup dried parsley	⅓ cup chili powder
⅓ cup dried minced onion	¼ cup ground cumin
¼ cup dried chives	¼ cup salt

In a large bowl, combine the spices and store in an airtight container.

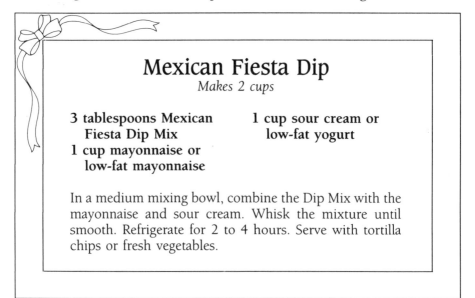

Mexican Fiesta Dip
Makes 2 cups

3 tablespoons Mexican Fiesta Dip Mix	1 cup sour cream or low-fat yogurt
1 cup mayonnaise or low-fat mayonnaise	

In a medium mixing bowl, combine the Dip Mix with the
mayonnaise and sour cream. Whisk the mixture until
smooth. Refrigerate for 2 to 4 hours. Serve with tortilla
chips or fresh vegetables.

Lemon Pepper Seasoning Mix

Makes 2 cups

L emon pepper adds a piquant flavor when used on grilled meats. Put this spice mixture into a Lucite shaker, pack it into a picnic basket with a tablecloth and napkins, fresh lemons, and some extra virgin olive oil for grilling.

1 cup ground black pepper
⅓ cup dried lemon peel
3 tablespoons coriander seeds

¼ cup dried minced onion
¼ cup dried thyme leaves

Stir all the ingredients together and store in airtight jars.

Grilled Lemon Chicken
Serves 4

¼ cup fresh lemon juice
¼ cup extra virgin olive oil

2 teaspoons Lemon Pepper Seasoning Mix
6 chicken cutlets

Preheat the broiler or barbecue grill. In a low flat dish, stir together the lemon juice, oil, and Lemon Pepper Seasoning Mix. Add the chicken breasts, and marinate in the refrigerator for 30 to 45 minutes. Grill over hot coals or broil for 4 minutes on each side, or until done. Serve hot or at room temperature.

Seasoned Salt Mix

Makes 1¼ cups

S easoned salt may be used in place of table salt in a clear salt-shaker. It makes a nice addition to a barbecue basket for Father's Day, or for a friend who has just built a new deck or patio. Fill a basket with a checkered tablecloth, barbecue tongs, an apron, mesquite wood chips, Seasoned Salt Mix, a recipe for your favorite grilled meat, and the recipe for grilled vegetables.

¾ cup salt
¼ cup garlic salt
1 teaspoon pepper
½ teaspoon oregano

1 teaspoon paprika
⅛ teaspoon celery seed
¼ teaspoon white pepper
¼ teaspoon dry mustard

Mix all the ingredients together in a glass bowl, and store in an airtight container.

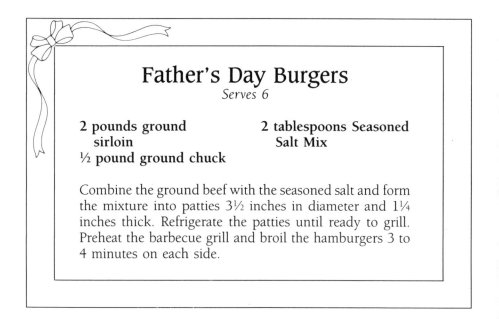

Father's Day Burgers
Serves 6

2 pounds ground
   sirloin
½ pound ground chuck

2 tablespoons Seasoned
   Salt Mix

Combine the ground beef with the seasoned salt and form the mixture into patties 3½ inches in diameter and 1¼ inches thick. Refrigerate the patties until ready to grill. Preheat the barbecue grill and broil the hamburgers 3 to 4 minutes on each side.

Grilled Vegetables
Serves 6

½ cup olive oil
¼ cup lemon juice
1 tablespoon Seasoned
   Salt Mix
2 Japanese eggplants,
   sliced into ½-inch-
   thick rounds
2 medium zucchini,
   sliced into ½-inch-
   thick rounds

4 assorted peppers
   (red, yellow, purple,
   and green), cored,
   seeded, and cut into
   quarters
2 Vidalia onions,
   quartered

In a large glass bowl, whisk together the oil, lemon juice, and Seasoned Salt Mix. Add the vegetables and marinate 2 hours. Reserve the marinade. Preheat the barbecue until the coals are glowing and have a white ash. If using a gas grill, preheat the grill for 10 minutes. Spray a barbecue basket or mesh grill rack with a nonstick coating such as Pam. Drain the vegetables and lay them into the basket or onto the grill rack. Grill the vegetables, shaking the basket frequently to turn them. Total cooking time should be 6 to 8 minutes. The vegetables are done when evenly browned and crisp-tender. Remove from the heat, and drizzle some of the reserved marinade over the vegetables. Serve hot or at room temperature. (You may substitute vegetables of your choice. Boil red or white new potatoes for 15 minutes before grilling. Quarter the boiled potatoes and grill as above.)

No-Salt Seasoned Salt Mix

Makes ½ cup

M any people cannot have salt in their diet, and this is just the seasoning they need to perk up any dinner. This spice is attractive when put into a Lucite saltshaker, or you could include it in a basket with soup and bread.

½ teaspoon garlic powder
¼ teaspoon thyme leaves
¼ teaspoon onion powder
¼ teaspoon paprika
⅛ teaspoon celery seed
¼ teaspoon white pepper

¼ teaspoon dry mustard
¼ teaspoon dried lemon peel
¼ teaspoon ground black pepper

Mix all the ingredients together in a small glass mixing bowl. Store in a covered container or in a cellophane bag.

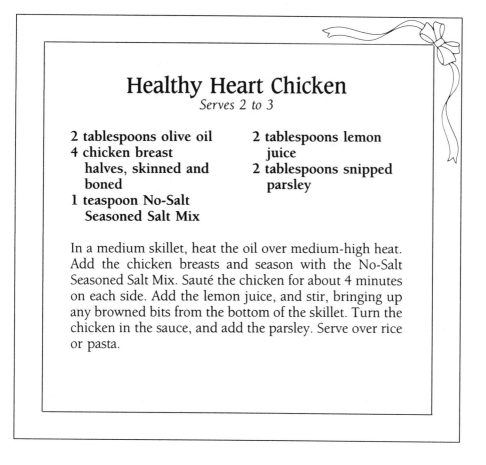

Healthy Heart Chicken
Serves 2 to 3

2 tablespoons olive oil
4 chicken breast halves, skinned and boned
1 teaspoon No-Salt Seasoned Salt Mix

2 tablespoons lemon juice
2 tablespoons snipped parsley

In a medium skillet, heat the oil over medium-high heat. Add the chicken breasts and season with the No-Salt Seasoned Salt Mix. Sauté the chicken for about 4 minutes on each side. Add the lemon juice, and stir, bringing up any browned bits from the bottom of the skillet. Turn the chicken in the sauce, and add the parsley. Serve over rice or pasta.

Caribbean Pepper Mix

Makes 1⅓ cups

N ot all peppercorns are the same. Soft green Malabar peppercorns are freeze-dried and have a crisp bite. Black Tellicherry peppercorns are rich in oils, and Muntok white peppercorns are aromatic. Combining the peppercorns with whole Jamaican allspice blends a taste of the Caribbean. Try this combination with the Peppered Steak using rum instead of the cognac.

½ cup Muntok white
  peppercorns
½ cup Tellicherry black
  peppercorns

¼ cup Malabar green
  peppercorns
2 tablespoons whole
  Jamaican allspice

In a large glass bowl, combine all the ingredients. Store in an airtight container.

Pepper Mill Combo Mix

Makes 2¼ cups

P resent this colorful peppercorn combination in a Lucite pepper mill, or in a long-necked bottle together with a wooden pepper mill. It can be given alone or with flavored oils and vinegars in a basket or in a wooden or Lucite salad bowl for a housewarming or bridal-shower gift. If you have trouble locating the suggested peppercorns, Select Origins is a great mail-order source (see Source Guide).

½ cup Muntok white
  peppercorns
½ cup Malabar green
  peppercorns

¼ cup red pepper flakes
1 cup Tellicherry or
  Malabar black
  peppercorns

Mix all the ingredients together in a glass bowl, and fill the pepper mill.

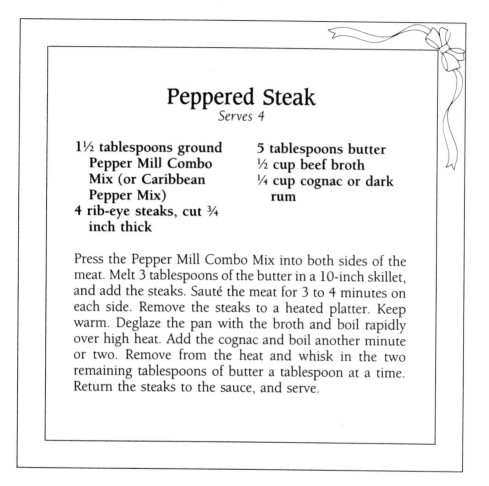

Peppered Steak

Serves 4

1½ tablespoons ground
  Pepper Mill Combo
  Mix (or Caribbean
  Pepper Mix)
4 rib-eye steaks, cut ¾
  inch thick

5 tablespoons butter
½ cup beef broth
¼ cup cognac or dark
  rum

Press the Pepper Mill Combo Mix into both sides of the meat. Melt 3 tablespoons of the butter in a 10-inch skillet, and add the steaks. Sauté the meat for 3 to 4 minutes on each side. Remove the steaks to a heated platter. Keep warm. Deglaze the pan with the broth and boil rapidly over high heat. Add the cognac and boil another minute or two. Remove from the heat and whisk in the two remaining tablespoons of butter a tablespoon at a time. Return the steaks to the sauce, and serve.

Bouquet Garni Mix

Makes 2½ cups

B ouquets garnis are little packets of herbs, traditionally wrapped in squares of cheesecloth, which are added to soups and stews. These can be given in an airtight spice jar or you can pack Bouquet Garni Mix into ceramic casseroles or soup tureens. This mix is a great gift during the Thanksgiving and Christmas holidays when your friends are making soups and stews from leftover turkey.

½ cup parsley
½ cup dried thyme
½ cup bay leaves

½ cup sage
½ cup rosemary

Crush the herbs in a glass bowl. Pack one tablespoon into each cheesecloth bag and tie the bags with twine. Store the bags in an airtight container.

Turkey Soup
Serves 8

2 to 4 quarts raw or
  cooked turkey or
  chicken bones and
  scraps (I use the
  whole turkey
  carcass)
Water to cover by
  1 inch
1 tablespoon salt

1 medium onion,
  chopped
½ cup chopped carrot
2 ribs celery, chopped
1 Bouquet Garni Mix
½ cup each chopped
  celery, carrot, and
  onion (reserved)

Chop the carcass into 2-inch pieces, and place in a 5-to 6-quart stockpot with the water, salt, vegetables, and seasonings. Bring the mixture to the boil, and skim off the gray scum that will rise. Reduce the heat, so that the soup is at a simmer. Partially cover the pan and simmer for 2 hours. Strain the stock into a large bowl. Allow the soup to stand for 15 minutes. Skim off the fat from the top of the soup, and return the soup to a saucepan. Remove as much turkey meat from the carcass as possible and cut the meat into 1-inch chunks. Add the reserved vegetables to the soup and bring the soup to a boil. Reduce the heat and simmer for 15 minutes. Add 2 cups of the turkey meat, and heat through. Serve the soup with crusty bread.

Herbes de Provence Mix

Makes 1¼ cups

A combination of French thyme, oregano, rosemary, and basil, herbes de Provence are used in the Mediterranean region of Provence in France. Herbes de Provence Mix can be used when sautéing vegetables, in grilling or baking poultry, or on pizza. They are traditionally stored in earthenware crocks, or you can use airtight jars. Pack these spices in a basket with Pizza Dough Mix (see page 88) or French Baguette Mix (see page 71). Herbes de Provence Mix can be given in a large-handled basket lined with a quilted table runner, and combined with some fresh vegetables from your garden for a ratatouille. Make sure to include eggplant, summer squash, and fresh tomatoes.

½ cup whole dried thyme
¼ cup whole dried basil
2 tablespoons whole
   dried oregano

2 tablespoons whole
   dried rosemary

In a medium glass bowl, combine all the spices and stir until thoroughly mixed. Store in an airtight container.

Ratatouille

Serves 8

⅓ cup olive oil
1 large onion, sliced
1 green pepper, sliced
3 large garlic cloves,
  minced
3 medium zucchini, cut
  into ½-inch slices
3 medium Japanese
  eggplants, cut into
  ½-inch slices

2 cups chopped
  tomatoes, peeled,
  seeded, and juiced
1 tablespoon Herbes de
  Provence Mix
¼ cup grated Parmesan
  cheese, mixed with
  ¼ cup grated Swiss
  cheese

Preheat the broiler. Pour the olive oil into a 12-inch skillet, and heat over medium-high heat. Add the onion, pepper, and garlic, and sauté for 3 to 4 minutes, until the vegetables are crisp but tender. Remove the vegetables from the skillet, leaving some of the oil in the pan. Add the zucchini and eggplant, and sauté for 2 to 3 minutes, tossing until the vegetables become tender. Add the onion-pepper mixture, stirring over moderate heat. Add the tomatoes, and cook about 4 minutes until the juices have almost boiled off. Add the Herbes Mix, and toss well. Transfer the mixture to a buttered 1-quart casserole, and cover with the Parmesan-Swiss cheese mixture. Broil for 3 to 5 minutes, until the cheese is golden. Serve with grilled meats or fish.

Tarragon Mustard Blend

Makes 1 cup

T arragon Mustard Blend is a delicious addition to salad dressings, dips, chicken marinades, and mayonnaise. Pack this herb mixture in a spice jar and tuck it into a salad spinner with a muslin lettuce bag, a clove of elephant garlic, some olive oil, and wine vinegar.

½ cup dried minced
    onion
¼ cup dried whole
    tarragon
2 tablespoons dry
    mustard

1 teaspoon black pepper
1 teaspoon fennel seed
1 teaspoon dried savory

Stir the spices together in a small bowl and store in airtight jars.

Tarragon Mustard Blend Vinaigrette

Makes 1½ cups

1 cup olive oil
⅓ cup white wine
  vinegar
2 tablespoons Tarragon
  Mustard Blend

1 teaspoon salt
1 clove crushed garlic

In a large glass bowl, whisk together the oil, vinegar, herb mixture, salt, and garlic. Store in the refrigerator until ready to use. Toss with mixed greens.

Tarragon Mayonnaise Sauce

Makes 1⅓ cups

1 cup mayonnaise or
  low-fat mayonnaise
⅓ cup sour cream or
  low-fat yogurt

3 tablespoons Tarragon
  Mustard Blend

In a small bowl, whisk the mayonnaise, sour cream, and herb mixture until the herbs are distributed. Cover and refrigerate 2 hours, or overnight. Serve as a dip for fresh vegetables, topping for baked potatoes, or a sauce for grilled fish or vegetables.

Cajun Seasoning Mix

Makes ⅔ cup

C ajun seasoning can be put into a basket along with a small bottle of good-quality olive oil, Dillweed Dip Mix (see page 4), Shrimp Jambalaya Mix (see page 56), and Double-Fudge Brownie Mix (see page 92), and it becomes a "meal kit." This versatile spice mixture can also be given in a small earthenware jar with a bottle of extra virgin olive oil, and French Baguette Mix (see page 71).

3 tablespoons salt
1 tablespoon paprika
1 tablespoon onion
  powder
1 tablespoon garlic
  powder
1 tablespoon cayenne
  pepper

½ teaspoon white pepper
1½ teaspoons whole
  thyme
¾ teaspoon black pepper
½ teaspoon whole
  oregano

Combine all the ingredients in a large bowl. Place in an airtight jar or container.

Barbecued Cajun Salmon
Serves 4

3 tablespoons Cajun
  Seasoning Mix
⅓ cup olive oil

2 pounds salmon fillets
  or steaks

Mix the Cajun Seasoning Mix and olive oil in a shallow dish large enough to hold the fish. Marinate the salmon steaks in the mixture for about 20 minutes, coating thoroughly. Barbecue the salmon over hot coals, using 10 minutes total cooking time for each 1-inch thickness of the fish.

Spiced Shrimp
Serves 8

4 cups water
2 tablespoons lemon
  juice
2 tablespoons Cajun
  Seasoning Mix

1 pound large shrimp,
  peeled and deveined

In a 3-quart saucepan, bring the water, lemon juice, and Cajun Seasoning Mix to a boil. Add the shrimp, bring back to a boil, and remove from the heat. Let stand 5 minutes. Drain the shrimp, refrigerate, and serve cold with cocktail sauce.

Artichoke Spice Mix

Makes ⅔ cup

An unusual springtime gift. Include this spice mixture in a basket with four artichokes and four ceramic artichoke plates. If you prefer to give fresh lemon and garlic, amend the gift tag directions to include 1 teaspoon fresh lemon peel and 1 garlic clove, cut into quarters.

¼ cup dried lemon peel
2 tablespoons celery seed
1 tablespoon dried thyme leaves

3 tablespoons garlic salt
3 crushed bay leaves

Combine all the ingredients in a bowl, and store in an airtight container.

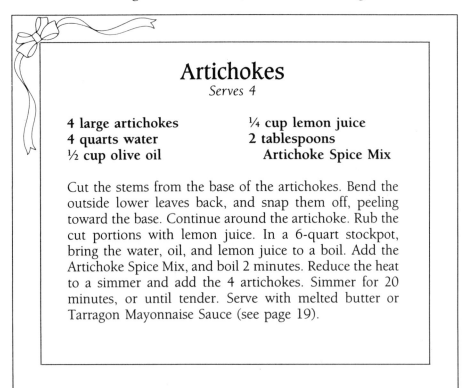

Artichokes

Serves 4

4 large artichokes
4 quarts water
½ cup olive oil

¼ cup lemon juice
2 tablespoons Artichoke Spice Mix

Cut the stems from the base of the artichokes. Bend the outside lower leaves back, and snap them off, peeling toward the base. Continue around the artichoke. Rub the cut portions with lemon juice. In a 6-quart stockpot, bring the water, oil, and lemon juice to a boil. Add the Artichoke Spice Mix, and boil 2 minutes. Reduce the heat to a simmer and add the 4 artichokes. Simmer for 20 minutes, or until tender. Serve with melted butter or Tarragon Mayonnaise Sauce (see page 19).

Soup Mixes

A bowl of homemade soup is warming and satisfying. Soup fills a home with aromas that lead us to the kitchen for a bowl of comfort. These mixes are welcome gifts that, with the addition of a few simple ingredients, provide an opportunity to enjoy a homemade soup. Each one can be given in a cellophane bag with directions attached, or they can be packed in glass jars or a pretty soup tureen. Large baskets can be filled with soup mix, soup mugs, crackers, croutons, or bread, and a ladle for serving. Soup mixes make colorful gifts when layered in glass jars. My children make them at Christmastime to give to their teachers. They're also terrific as stocking stuffers. Or fill a soup pot with an assortment of soup mixes in resealable plastic bags, each wrapped in a different colorful gift paper with recipes attached with ribbons.

Since some soups are also tasty served chilled, for summer gifts, combine appropriate soup mixes with big-handled acrylic mugs, ideal for patio or poolside entertaining.

Black Bean Soup Mix

Makes 2¼ cups

T he basis of a spicy Caribbean-style soup, this mix will be a welcome change of pace for your friends. Since the beans are soaked overnight, you will need to package them separately from the spice mixture. Put the beans in a glass jar, and pack the spice mix into a small spice jar. Give the mixes in a colorful straw beach-type basket with a package of California Corn Bread Mix (see page 68) and a Bob Marley reggae tape. (I call it music to cook by.)

1 pound dried black
   beans
½ teaspoon black pepper
1 bay leaf
1 teaspoon dried thyme
   leaves

1 teaspoon cumin powder
4 beef bouillon cubes,
   crumbled

Place the black beans into an airtight container. Combine the spices and bouillon in a small bowl, and stir until blended. Place the spice mix in an airtight container.

Black Bean Soup
Serves 8

1 pound dried black beans
2 tablespoons vegetable oil
1 medium onion, chopped
½ pound Polish sausage

1 package Black Bean
  Soup Mix
8 cups water
Salt and pepper

In a stockpot, soak the beans in water overnight. Drain the beans and reserve. In a large stockpot, heat the oil, and add the onion and Polish sausage. Sauté the mixture over medium-high heat, until the onion is translucent. Add the beans and Black Bean Soup Mix. Stir the mixture, and add the water. Reduce the heat to a simmer, and cook partially covered for 2 hours. Season to taste with salt and pepper.

Split Pea Soup Mix

Makes 2½ cups

T his is an attractive mix of green and yellow split peas with red
lentils. Pack this mix into a glass jar and include it in a basket
with Honey Whole Wheat Bread Mix (see page 72) and Mulled Cider
Mix (see page 119). If available, include a fresh thyme plant in the
basket. Omit the dried thyme from the mix and amend the gift tag instructions to include 2 teaspoons snipped thyme added with the water.

1 pound green split peas	½ teaspoon pepper
¼ cup red lentils	1 teaspoon dried thyme
¼ cup yellow split peas	1 bay leaf
2 teaspoons salt	

Combine all the ingredients in a medium bowl and stir until blended.
Store in an airtight container.

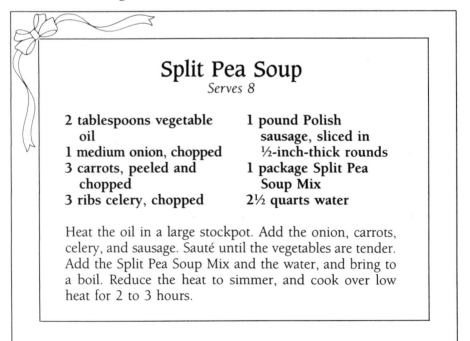

Split Pea Soup

Serves 8

2 tablespoons vegetable oil	1 pound Polish sausage, sliced in ½-inch-thick rounds
1 medium onion, chopped	
3 carrots, peeled and chopped	1 package Split Pea Soup Mix
3 ribs celery, chopped	2½ quarts water

Heat the oil in a large stockpot. Add the onion, carrots,
celery, and sausage. Sauté until the vegetables are tender.
Add the Split Pea Soup Mix and the water, and bring to
a boil. Reduce the heat to simmer, and cook over low
heat for 2 to 3 hours.

Turkey Noodle Soup Mix

Makes 1⅛ cups

T his is a great way to use leftover holiday turkey. Pack the mix into a turkey or chicken soup tureen, or with soup bowls decorated with turkeys or chickens for a great hostess gift during the holidays.

1 cup uncooked fine egg
  noodles
1½ tablespoons chicken-
  flavored bouillon
  granules
½ teaspoon ground black
  pepper

¼ teaspoon dried whole
  thyme
⅛ teaspoon celery seeds
⅛ teaspoon garlic powder
1 bay leaf

Combine all the ingredients in a medium bowl. Store in an airtight container.

Turkey Noodle Soup
Serves 8

1 package Turkey
  Noodle Soup Mix
8 cups water
2 carrots, diced

2 stalks celery, diced
¼ cup minced onion
3 cups cooked, diced
  turkey

Combine the Turkey Noodle Soup Mix and the water in a large stockpot. Add the carrots, celery, and onion, and bring to a boil. Cover the soup and reduce the heat to a simmer. Simmer for 15 minutes. Discard the bay leaf. Stir in the turkey and simmer an additional 5 minutes.

World's Best
Bean Soup Mix

Makes 40 cups

I am often asked why this soup is named the World's Best Bean ` Soup. My reply is that it is inexpensive, makes an enormous quantity for gift giving, and the soup is colorful and delicious. This mix will make twenty 2-cup packages. Stored in glass jars, canisters, cellophane bags, or plastic bags, twisted airtight and put into a soup tureen, or into a basket with soup bowls and soup spoons, this mix makes an outstanding gift.

Include fresh garlic and onion in your basket.

1 pound navy beans	1 pound yellow split peas
1 pound Great Northern beans	1 pound green split peas
1 pound dried pinto beans	1 pound black-eyed peas
1 pound red beans	1 pound dried lentils
1 pound dried soybeans	1 pound dried large limas
	1 pound dried baby limas
	1 pound barley pearls

Combine all the ingredients in a large pan or bowl. Measure out 2-cup gift packages, and store in airtight containers.

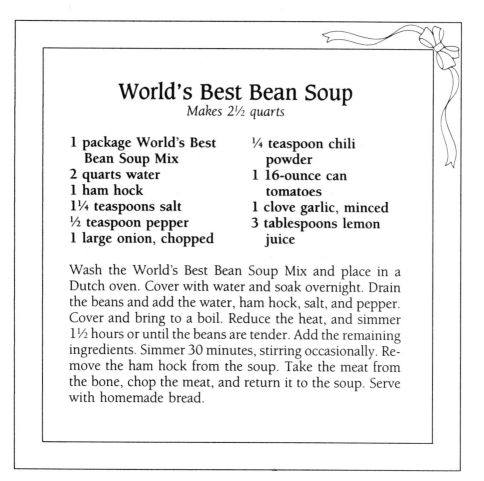

World's Best Bean Soup
Makes 2½ quarts

1 package World's Best Bean Soup Mix	¼ teaspoon chili powder
2 quarts water	1 16-ounce can tomatoes
1 ham hock	1 clove garlic, minced
1¼ teaspoons salt	3 tablespoons lemon juice
½ teaspoon pepper	
1 large onion, chopped	

Wash the World's Best Bean Soup Mix and place in a Dutch oven. Cover with water and soak overnight. Drain the beans and add the water, ham hock, salt, and pepper. Cover and bring to a boil. Reduce the heat, and simmer 1½ hours or until the beans are tender. Add the remaining ingredients. Simmer 30 minutes, stirring occasionally. Remove the ham hock from the soup. Take the meat from the bone, chop the meat, and return it to the soup. Serve with homemade bread.

New Orleans Gumbo Mix

Makes ¾ cup

T his recipe is so easy and the results are spectacular. Pack this into a stockpot with a package of French Baguette Mix (see page 71). Include a bottle of Louisiana hot sauce and a jar of filé powder.

2 teaspoons garlic salt
1 teaspoon white pepper
1 teaspoon ground black pepper
½ teaspoon dried oregano
1 teaspoon ground allspice
1 teaspoon cayenne pepper

2 teaspoons dried thyme leaves
¼ teaspoon ground cloves
2 bay leaves
6 chicken bouillon cubes
½ cup flour

Stir the ingredients in a medium bowl, and store in an airtight container.

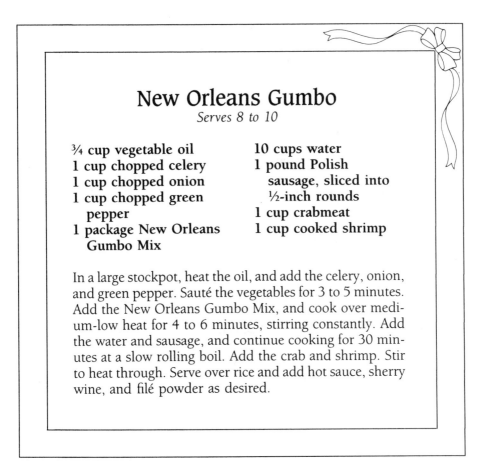

New Orleans Gumbo
Serves 8 to 10

¾ cup vegetable oil
1 cup chopped celery
1 cup chopped onion
1 cup chopped green
  pepper
1 package New Orleans
  Gumbo Mix

10 cups water
1 pound Polish
  sausage, sliced into
  ½-inch rounds
1 cup crabmeat
1 cup cooked shrimp

In a large stockpot, heat the oil, and add the celery, onion, and green pepper. Sauté the vegetables for 3 to 5 minutes. Add the New Orleans Gumbo Mix, and cook over medium-low heat for 4 to 6 minutes, stirring constantly. Add the water and sausage, and continue cooking for 30 minutes at a slow rolling boil. Add the crab and shrimp. Stir to heat through. Serve over rice and add hot sauce, sherry wine, and filé powder as desired.

Chili Mix

Makes ½ cup

C hili is a great warm-up on a cold winter evening. This mix can be given in a porcelain chili pot with chili bowls, California Corn Bread Mix (see page 68), or tortilla chips. Include a Vidalia onion for garnishing the chili.

2 teaspoons ground
  cumin
2 teaspoons dried oregano
½ teaspoon salt
½ teaspoon cayenne
  pepper

2 teaspoons onion
  powder
½ teaspoon garlic salt
⅓ cup masa harina

In a small bowl, combine all the ingredients and stir until blended. Store in an airtight container.

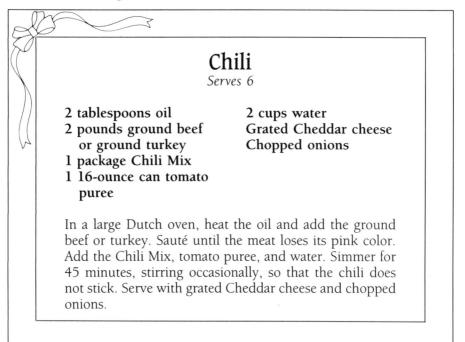

Chili

Serves 6

2 tablespoons oil
2 pounds ground beef
  or ground turkey
1 package Chili Mix
1 16-ounce can tomato
  puree

2 cups water
Grated Cheddar cheese
Chopped onions

In a large Dutch oven, heat the oil and add the ground beef or turkey. Sauté until the meat loses its pink color. Add the Chili Mix, tomato puree, and water. Simmer for 45 minutes, stirring occasionally, so that the chili does not stick. Serve with grated Cheddar cheese and chopped onions.

Fitz-Patrick's Boston Baked Beans Mix

Makes 2¼ cups

My father's favorite Saturday night dinner was Boston baked beans with brown bread. Pack this mix into a baked-bean crock with a jar of molasses and Mom's Heirloom Brown Bread Mix (see page 69).

2 cups small white pea beans
½ teaspoon dried thyme
1 bay leaf
¼ teaspoon ground ginger
½ teaspoon ground pepper
1½ teaspoons salt

Combine the ingredients in a medium bowl. Stir until the mixture is blended, and pack it into an airtight container.

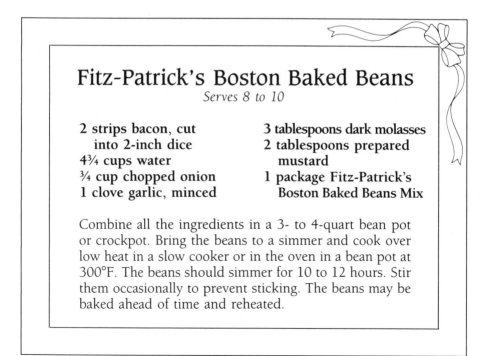

Fitz-Patrick's Boston Baked Beans

Serves 8 to 10

2 strips bacon, cut into 2-inch dice
4¾ cups water
¾ cup chopped onion
1 clove garlic, minced
3 tablespoons dark molasses
2 tablespoons prepared mustard
1 package Fitz-Patrick's Boston Baked Beans Mix

Combine all the ingredients in a 3- to 4-quart bean pot or crockpot. Bring the beans to a simmer and cook over low heat in a slow cooker or in the oven in a bean pot at 300°F. The beans should simmer for 10 to 12 hours. Stir them occasionally to prevent sticking. The beans may be baked ahead of time and reheated.

Minestrone Soup Mix

Makes 2 cups

T he ingredients for this minestrone soup are packed into two different containers, and can be added to a basket with a bottle of Italian red wine, a chunk of Parmigian-Reggiano cheese, and a loaf of crusty Italian bread.

¼ cup dried split peas
½ cup dried kidney beans
4 crumbled beef bouillon
   cubes
1 teaspoon dried basil

1 teaspoon dried oregano
1 teaspoon dried parsley
1½ teaspoons salt
½ teaspoon ground pepper
1 cup elbow macaroni

Combine the peas, beans, boullion, and spices in a bowl. Stir to blend and store in an airtight container. Place the macaroni in an airtight container.

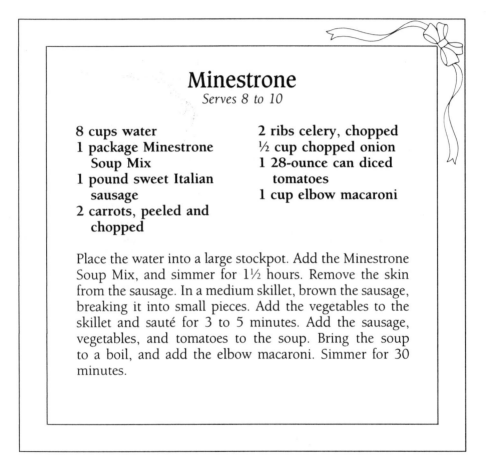

Minestrone
Serves 8 to 10

8 cups water
1 package Minestrone
  Soup Mix
1 pound sweet Italian
  sausage
2 carrots, peeled and
  chopped

2 ribs celery, chopped
½ cup chopped onion
1 28-ounce can diced
  tomatoes
1 cup elbow macaroni

Place the water into a large stockpot. Add the Minestrone Soup Mix, and simmer for 1½ hours. Remove the skin from the sausage. In a medium skillet, brown the sausage, breaking it into small pieces. Add the vegetables to the skillet and sauté for 3 to 5 minutes. Add the sausage, vegetables, and tomatoes to the soup. Bring the soup to a boil, and add the elbow macaroni. Simmer for 30 minutes.

Cajun Corn and Shrimp Soup Mix

Makes ⅓ cup

W ith a few additions, this soup starter becomes an elegant cream soup fit for a banquet table. Pack this into a summertime basket with 6 ears of fresh corn and French Baguette Mix (see page 71).

½ teaspoon salt
½ teaspoon cayenne
  pepper
1 tablespoon sweet
  paprika
2¾ teaspoons garlic
  powder
2 teaspoons ground black
  pepper

1½ teaspoons onion
  powder
1½ teaspoons dried
  oregano leaves
1½ teaspoons dried
  thyme leaves
5 vegetable bouillon
  cubes, crumbled

In a medium bowl, stir the mixture together. Store the soup mix in an airtight container.

Cajun Corn and Shrimp Soup

Serves 8

½ cup butter
1 medium onion,
  chopped
¼ cup flour
1 tablespoon Cajun
  Corn and Shrimp
  Soup Mix
3 cups boiling water

3 cups fresh corn
  kernels, scraped
  from the cob, or
  equivalent frozen
  defrosted corn
¾ pound medium
  peeled and deveined
  shrimp
½ cup heavy cream

In a large saucepan, melt the butter and add the chopped onion. Sauté for 3 minutes. Add the flour, and cook, whisking constantly. Stir the soup mix into the flour and gradually add the boiling water, whisking until the mixture is thick. Add the corn and shrimp, and simmer for 5 minutes, or until the shrimp are pink. Whisk in the heavy cream. Continue to cook over low heat, until the soup is heated through.

Beef Vegetable and Barley Soup Starter Mix

Makes 1⅛ cups

T his hearty soup makes an unusual presentation when served in individual round sourdough loaves. A versatile mix, it can also be made into a vegetarian soup if you substitute vegetable bouillon for the beef bouillon and omit the stew meat. A chicken soup can be made by substituting chicken bouillon and 1 pound of diced chicken meat for the beef.

Give this mix in a large basket with 2 round loaves of bread, a bottle of red wine, and an assortment of cheeses.

½ cup barley
½ cup dried split peas
3 beef bouillon cubes, crumbled
¼ teaspoon ground black pepper

½ teaspoon dried whole basil
¼ teaspoon dried whole oregano
1 bay leaf

Combine the ingredients in a small bowl, and store in an airtight container.

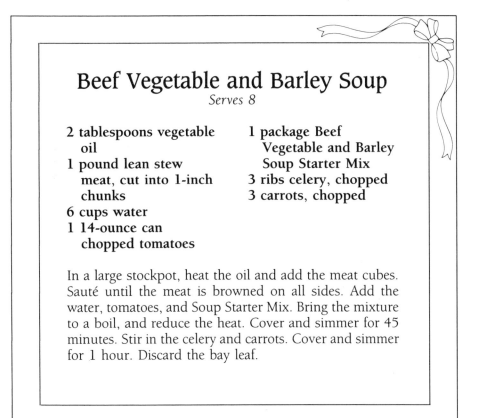

Beef Vegetable and Barley Soup
Serves 8

2 tablespoons vegetable
  oil
1 pound lean stew
  meat, cut into 1-inch
  chunks
6 cups water
1 14-ounce can
  chopped tomatoes

1 package Beef
  Vegetable and Barley
  Soup Starter Mix
3 ribs celery, chopped
3 carrots, chopped

In a large stockpot, heat the oil and add the meat cubes.
Sauté until the meat is browned on all sides. Add the
water, tomatoes, and Soup Starter Mix. Bring the mixture
to a boil, and reduce the heat. Cover and simmer for 45
minutes. Stir in the celery and carrots. Cover and simmer
for 1 hour. Discard the bay leaf.

Lentil Soup Mix

Makes 2¼ cups

My grandmother used to make this soup and serve it with her homemade bread. This is a savory reminder of her kitchen. Give this mix in a basket, packed in a cellophane bag, with a soup ladle and French Baguette Mix (see page 71).

2 cups dried lentils	**½ teaspoon dried thyme**
3 chicken bouillon cubes, crumbled	**½ teaspoon garlic powder**

In a medium bowl, stir all the ingredients together. Store the soup in an airtight container.

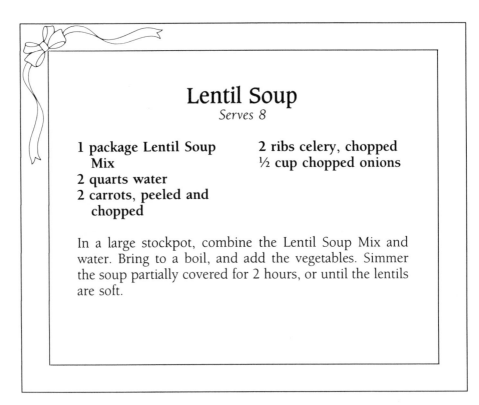

Lentil Soup
Serves 8

1 package Lentil Soup Mix	**2 ribs celery, chopped**
2 quarts water	**½ cup chopped onions**
2 carrots, peeled and chopped	

In a large stockpot, combine the Lentil Soup Mix and water. Bring to a boil, and add the vegetables. Simmer the soup partially covered for 2 hours, or until the lentils are soft.

Rice Mixes

Rice mixes can be a lifesaver to a friend or hostess, especially during busy holiday seasons. Each mix makes enough for six to eight servings, and is a delightful addition to any meal basket, as well as a lovely gift all by itself.

There are several different varieties of rice that can be used to create delicious mixes. Wild rice is the seed of an aquatic grass that is grown primarily in northern Minnesota. It has a chewy texture, and complements pork, duck, chicken, turkey, and game hens. Imported Italian arborio rice has short fat grains, and can absorb a great deal of liquid. Arborio rice is used primarily in risottos, which go well with sauced meats, such as osso bucco. Brown rice is healthful and a bit chewy, adds a nutlike flavor, and is delicious when served with lamb or chicken. Basmati rice is aromatic and full of flavor, and cooks like long-grain rice.

I like to pack the mixes in cellophane bags and nest them in a large lotus bowl. Wrap the bowl in colored cellophane and you have a gift for less than ten dollars. For a housewarming or shower gift, give rice mixes in an overproof casserole with a lid. Since the rice mixes have a variety of colors, layering the ingredients in glass jars also makes a nice presentation. A basket filled with a variety of rice mixes makes a sensational housewarming or shower gift.

Fruited Rice Mix

Makes 2¼ cups

A gourmet treat flavored with orange and apricot, this mix is deceptively simple, and a fancy side dish for any meal. Give this rice mix wrapped in a cellophane bag, and place it inside a 1½-quart ovenproof casserole. Wrap the casserole in colored cellophane and tie with ribbons.

1 cup long-grain rice
½ cup finely chopped
    dried apricots
¼ cup raisins
¼ cup slivered almonds
1 chicken bouillon cube,
    crumbled

2 teaspoons dried parsley
1½ teaspoons dried
    orange rind
½ teaspoon onion powder

Combine all the ingredients in a medium bowl. Stir to blend, and store in an airtight container.

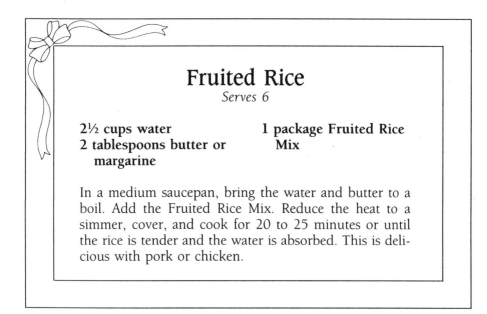

Fruited Rice

Serves 6

2½ cups water
2 tablespoons butter or
    margarine

1 package Fruited Rice
    Mix

In a medium saucepan, bring the water and butter to a boil. Add the Fruited Rice Mix. Reduce the heat to a simmer, cover, and cook for 20 to 25 minutes or until the rice is tender and the water is absorbed. This is delicious with pork or chicken.

Raisin Curried Wild Rice Mix

Makes 1¾ cups

T he perfect accompaniment for sautéed chicken or broiled Cornish game hens. Present this rice mix layered in a glass jar, and tie ribbons to the neck of the jar.

1 cup wild rice
4 chicken bouillon cubes, crumbled
3 tablespoons dried minced onion

½ cup raisins
½ teaspoon curry powder

In a glass jar that holds 1¾ cups, pour the rice into the bottom. Layer the rest of the ingredients in the order given.

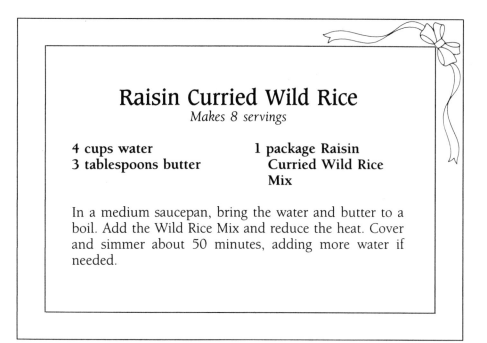

Raisin Curried Wild Rice
Makes 8 servings

4 cups water
3 tablespoons butter

1 package Raisin Curried Wild Rice Mix

In a medium saucepan, bring the water and butter to a boil. Add the Wild Rice Mix and reduce the heat. Cover and simmer about 50 minutes, adding more water if needed.

Drunken Wild Rice Mix

Makes 1⅓ cups

T his elegant rice dish has a surprising addition of brandy at the very end of the cooking time. For packaging, if you sew, you can easily whip up a drawstring bag made of pretty patterned cotton fabric, line it with a resealable plastic bag, and fill with Drunken Wild Rice Mix. Place the bag in a basket with a 4-ounce bottle of brandy and 6 rice bowls.

⅓ cup dried currants
⅔ cup wild rice
2 chicken bouillon cubes,
   crumbled

⅓ cup chopped pecans

Combine all the ingredients in a medium bowl. Stir until the ingredients are blended. Store in an airtight container.

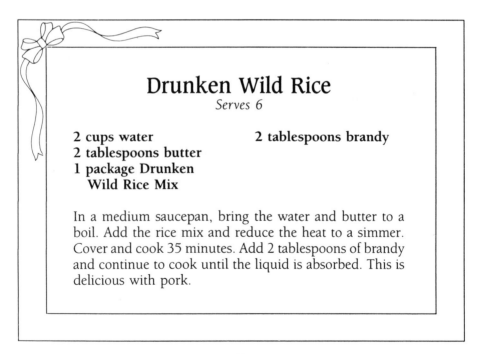

Drunken Wild Rice

Serves 6

2 cups water
2 tablespoons butter
1 package Drunken
   Wild Rice Mix

2 tablespoons brandy

In a medium saucepan, bring the water and butter to a boil. Add the rice mix and reduce the heat to a simmer. Cover and cook 35 minutes. Add 2 tablespoons of brandy and continue to cook until the liquid is absorbed. This is delicious with pork.

Orange Blossom Rice Mix

Makes 1⅛ cups

F ragrant with orange and hints of marjoram and thyme, this rice
mix makes a nice presentation in lotus bowls. Pack the mix in
a cellophane bag, and nest 4 small lotus bowls into a large lotus bowl.
Place the mix in the top bowl, add 4 sets of chopsticks, and wrap the
gift in Oriental-patterned gift paper or Chinese newspaper.

1 cup uncooked long-
  grain white rice
½ teaspoon dried orange
  peel

1 teaspoon salt
¼ teaspoon dried
  marjoram
¼ teaspoon dried thyme

Combine all the ingredients in a medium bowl. Store in an airtight
container.

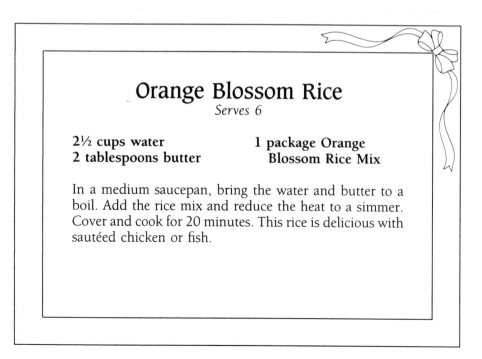

Orange Blossom Rice
Serves 6

2½ cups water
2 tablespoons butter

1 package Orange
  Blossom Rice Mix

In a medium saucepan, bring the water and butter to a
boil. Add the rice mix and reduce the heat to a simmer.
Cover and cook for 20 minutes. This rice is delicious with
sautéed chicken or fish.

Curried Rice Mix

Makes 1⅓ cups

T his curried rice mix is an interesting complement for plain chicken or pork. I like to layer Curried Rice Mix in a glass jar, and pack it into a basket along with a jar of mango chutney.

1 cup long-grain rice
1 chicken bouillon cube, crumbled
2 tablespoons dried minced onion

¼ cup raisins
½ teaspoon curry powder

Layer the ingredients in the order given in a 1½-cup jar.

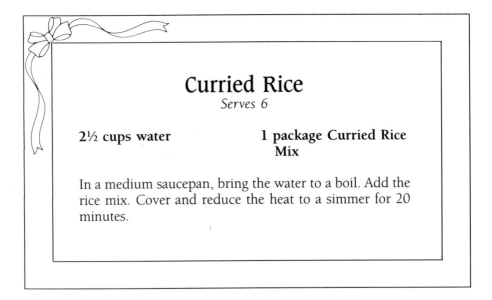

Curried Rice

Serves 6

2½ cups water

1 package Curried Rice Mix

In a medium saucepan, bring the water to a boil. Add the rice mix. Cover and reduce the heat to a simmer for 20 minutes.

Honey Nut Rice Mix

Makes 1⅔ cups

T he crunchy roasted peanuts and cinnamon flavor make this rice dish a hit with children. I like to give this in a basket with a jar of honey and a porcelain rice serving bowl.

1 cup long-grain rice
½ cup roasted peanuts
1 teaspoon cinnamon

¾ teaspoon ground ginger
1 chicken bouillon cube,
   crumbled

Combine all the ingredients in a medium bowl. Store in an airtight container.

Honey Nut Rice
Serves 6

¼ cup butter
¼ cup honey
2 cups water

1 package Honey Nut
   Rice Mix

In a medium saucepan, bring the butter, honey, and water to a boil. Add the Honey Nut Rice Mix. Cover and simmer over medium heat for 20 minutes. Excellent with turkey, ham, or pork.

Curried Rice with Fruit Mix

Makes 2½ cups

An appetizing side dish to serve with grilled chicken. Layer this mix into a cellophane bag or a glass jar, then give it in a basket with rice bowls, chopsticks, and chopstick rests.

1½ cups white rice
2¼ teaspoons curry powder
2 chicken bouillon cubes, crumbled
⅓ cup mixed dried fruits

½ cup slivered almonds
1½ tablespoons instant minced onion
3 tablespoons golden raisins

Layer the ingredients in the order given in an airtight container.

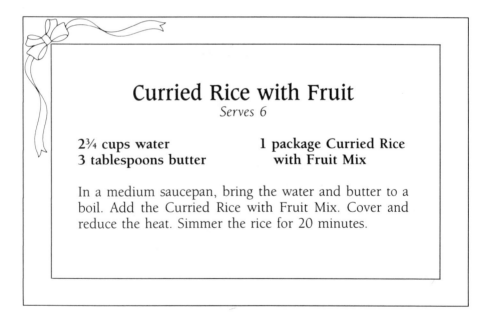

Curried Rice with Fruit

Serves 6

2¾ cups water
3 tablespoons butter

1 package Curried Rice with Fruit Mix

In a medium saucepan, bring the water and butter to a boil. Add the Curried Rice with Fruit Mix. Cover and reduce the heat. Simmer the rice for 20 minutes.

Bulgur Risotto Mix

Makes 1¾ cups

T his is a change of pace from ordinary rice. Cracked wheat bulgur is found in the health food section of the supermarket. Give this mix in a basket with other rice mixes. Make sure to include Paella Mix (see page 52), Arborio Risotto Mix (see page 58), and Fruited Rice Mix (see page 42).

1 tablespoon dried
   minced onion
3 chicken bouillon cubes,
   crumbled
1 teaspoon dried chervil

1 teaspoon dried thyme
¼ teaspoon black pepper
1½ cups cracked wheat
   bulgur

Combine all the ingredients in a medium bowl. Store in an airtight container.

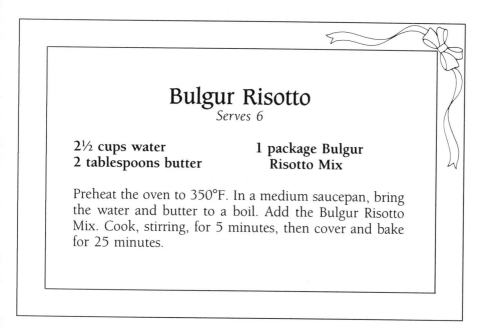

Bulgur Risotto
Serves 6

2½ cups water
2 tablespoons butter

1 package Bulgur
   Risotto Mix

Preheat the oven to 350°F. In a medium saucepan, bring the water and butter to a boil. Add the Bulgur Risotto Mix. Cook, stirring, for 5 minutes, then cover and bake for 25 minutes.

Savory Rice Blend Mix

Makes 1⅓ cups

This savory rice blend is beautiful layered in a glass jar and given with the fresh Barbecue Herb Basket (see page 132). Savory Rice provides a nice contrast to grilled meats.

1½ cups white rice
3 beef bouillon cubes,
   crumbled
¾ teaspoon dried rosemary

¾ teaspoon dried marjoram
¾ teaspoon dried thyme
2 teaspoons dried minced
   onion

Combine all the ingredients in a medium bowl. Store in an airtight container.

Savory Rice Blend
Serves 6

2½ cups water
2 tablespoons butter

1 package Savory Rice
Blend Mix

In a medium saucepan, bring the water and butter to a boil. Add the Savory Rice Blend Mix and reduce the heat. Cover and simmer for 20 minutes, until the liquid is absorbed and the rice is tender.

Syrian Rice Pilaf Mix

Makes 1⅓ cups

D elicious with chicken, seafood, or beef, this blend is similar to
the rice pilaf available on grocery shelves. I like to place this in
a basket with Cajun Seasoning Mix (see page 20), Tarragon Mustard
Blend (see page 18), and French Baguette Mix (see page 71) for a "Meal
Kit."

¼ cup orzo rice-shaped
  pasta
2 tablespoons dried
  minced onion
2 chicken bouillon cubes,
  crumbled

¼ teaspoon garlic powder
1 cup long-grain rice
¼ teaspoon turmeric

Combine the ingredients in a medium bowl, and stir to blend. Store
the rice mixture in an airtight container.

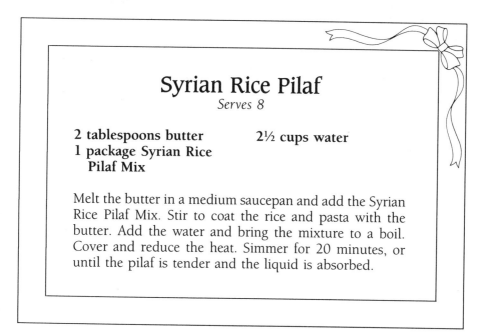

Syrian Rice Pilaf

Serves 8

2 tablespoons butter
1 package Syrian Rice
  Pilaf Mix

2½ cups water

Melt the butter in a medium saucepan and add the Syrian
Rice Pilaf Mix. Stir to coat the rice and pasta with the
butter. Add the water and bring the mixture to a boil.
Cover and reduce the heat. Simmer for 20 minutes, or
until the pilaf is tender and the liquid is absorbed.

Paella Mix

Makes 3¼ cups

Paella is the ultimate one-pot meal. It's easy to prepare and delicious to eat, with only one pot to wash. Give this mix wrapped in a cellophane bag, placed in a paella pan, along with a clove of elephant garlic, a small bottle of olive oil, a large fresh tomato, and a Vidalia onion. For an outer gift wrap, use crepe paper in pretty colors.

2 teaspoons salt
¼ teaspoon ground
  pepper
¼ teaspoon ground
  saffron

3 cups long-grain or
  arborio rice
4 chicken bouillon cubes,
  crumbled

Combine all the ingredients in a medium bowl. Store in an airtight container.

Paella

Serves 6

½ cup olive oil
1 2-pound chicken, cut
   into serving pieces
½ pound smoked
   sausage, cut into ½-
   inch rounds
½ cup sliced onions
2 cloves garlic, minced
1 medium red or green
   bell pepper, seeded
   and cut into strips

1 large tomato, peeled,
   seeded, and chopped
6 cups boiling water
1 package Paella Mix
½ pound raw peeled
   and deveined shrimp
12 hard-shelled clams
½ cup frozen petite
   peas

Preheat the oven to 400°F. In a 14-inch paella pan, sauté the chicken in the oil, turning the chicken until it is browned. Remove the chicken from the pan. Add the sausage, onion, garlic, pepper, and tomato. Sauté the mixture over medium-high heat until the vegetables are tender but crisp (about 4 minutes). Return the chicken to the pan, along with the Paella Mix. Pour in the water and bring to a boil. Taste the paella for seasoning, and adjust accordingly. Add the shrimp, clams, and peas, and bake, uncovered, for 25 to 30 minutes. Remove from the oven and let the paella rest for 10 minutes. Serve directly from the pan.

Red Beans and Rice Mix

Makes 2⅔ cups

T raditionally, red beans and rice are served for lunch on Mondays in New Orleans, but you can serve them any time. You will need to pack the beans, rice, and spice mix in separate containers. Place all three in a basket with French Baguette Mix (see page 71), Louisiana hot sauce, and a serving bowl. If you would like to substitute fresh garlic for the garlic powder, include the garlic in the basket, adding 1 clove of fresh chopped garlic to the ingredient list and recipe instructions.

½ pound dried small red
   beans
1 bay leaf
1 teaspoon salt
½ teaspoon dried thyme

½ teaspoon dried basil
1 teaspoon garlic powder
½ teaspoon dried parsley
¼ teaspoon cayenne
   pepper
2 cups long-grain white
   rice

Pack the beans in an airtight container.

Combine the whole bay leaf and spices in a small bowl, and store in an airtight container.

Place the rice in an airtight container.

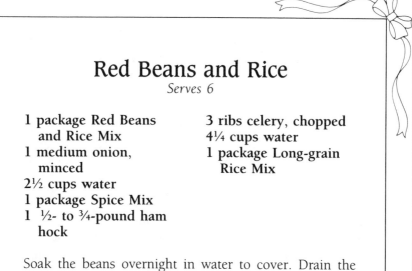

Red Beans and Rice
Serves 6

1 package Red Beans
  and Rice Mix
1 medium onion,
  minced
2½ cups water
1 package Spice Mix
1 ½- to ¾-pound ham
  hock

3 ribs celery, chopped
4¼ cups water
1 package Long-grain
  Rice Mix

Soak the beans overnight in water to cover. Drain the beans and place in a 4-quart saucepan. Add the onion, water, Spice Mix, ham hock, and celery. Bring the mixture to a boil, reduce the heat, and simmer gently about 2 hours, or until the beans are tender. Remove the ham hock, and chop the meat. Return the meat to the beans, and discard the bone. Remove the bay leaf from the beans. Keep the beans warm. In a 3-quart saucepan, heat the 4¼ cups of water to boiling. Add the Rice Mix, and simmer gently for 25 minutes, or until the water is absorbed. Stir the rice into the beans. Serve with Louisiana hot sauce.

Shrimp Jambalaya Mix

Makes 1¾ cups

Here's another one-pot meal that's a welcome addition to any cook's pantry. Place the Shrimp Jambalaya Mix and the separate rice mix in a basket with a wok or heat-proof serving container, pot holders, and an apron.

7 chicken bouillon cubes, crumbled
½ teaspoon dried thyme
1 bay leaf
½ teaspoon dried whole oregano
1½ cups raw converted rice
¼ teaspoon cayenne pepper
½ teaspoon dried basil
½ teaspoon ground black pepper

In a medium bowl combine the bouillon cubes and spices. Store the mixture in an airtight container.

Place the rice in an airtight container.

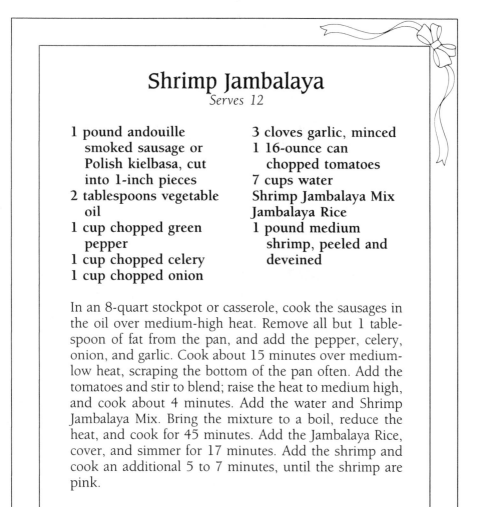

Shrimp Jambalaya
Serves 12

1 pound andouille
  smoked sausage or
  Polish kielbasa, cut
  into 1-inch pieces
2 tablespoons vegetable
  oil
1 cup chopped green
  pepper
1 cup chopped celery
1 cup chopped onion

3 cloves garlic, minced
1 16-ounce can
  chopped tomatoes
7 cups water
Shrimp Jambalaya Mix
Jambalaya Rice
1 pound medium
  shrimp, peeled and
  deveined

In an 8-quart stockpot or casserole, cook the sausages in
the oil over medium-high heat. Remove all but 1 tablespoon of fat from the pan, and add the pepper, celery,
onion, and garlic. Cook about 15 minutes over medium-
low heat, scraping the bottom of the pan often. Add the
tomatoes and stir to blend; raise the heat to medium high,
and cook about 4 minutes. Add the water and Shrimp
Jambalaya Mix. Bring the mixture to a boil, reduce the
heat, and cook for 45 minutes. Add the Jambalaya Rice,
cover, and simmer for 17 minutes. Add the shrimp and
cook an additional 5 to 7 minutes, until the shrimp are
pink.

Arborio Risotto Mix

Makes 2⅛ cups

R isotto is made with Italian arborio rice. Layer this mix in a glass jar with an airtight seal, and place it in a basket with a wedge of Parmigiana-Reggiano cheese, fresh shallots, and a bottle of red wine.

2 cups Italian arborio rice
4 chicken bouillon cubes,
  crumbled

⅓ teaspoon powdered
  saffron

Layer the ingredients in the order given in a selected container.

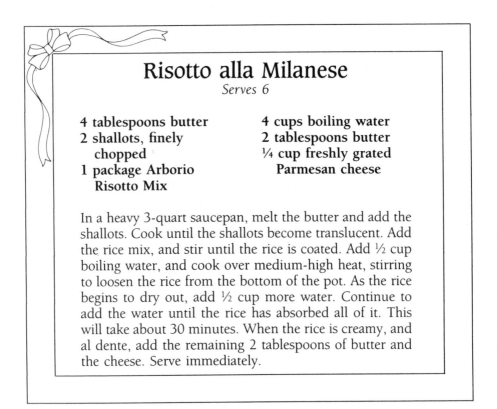

Risotto alla Milanese
Serves 6

4 tablespoons butter
2 shallots, finely
  chopped
1 package Arborio
  Risotto Mix

4 cups boiling water
2 tablespoons butter
¼ cup freshly grated
  Parmesan cheese

In a heavy 3-quart saucepan, melt the butter and add the shallots. Cook until the shallots become translucent. Add the rice mix, and stir until the rice is coated. Add ½ cup boiling water, and cook over medium-high heat, stirring to loosen the rice from the bottom of the pot. As the rice begins to dry out, add ½ cup more water. Continue to add the water until the rice has absorbed all of it. This will take about 30 minutes. When the rice is creamy, and al dente, add the remaining 2 tablespoons of butter and the cheese. Serve immediately.

Bread, Muffin, and Scone Mixes

T here is nothing more satisfying than taking a loaf of fresh baked bread from the oven. The mixes in this chapter will help your friends make a fine loaf of bread by simply adding a few additional ingredients. Also included in this chapter are some delicious muffin mixes and a scone mix.

When making bread mixes, I like to use a glass mixing bowl and a wire whisk to blend the ingredients together. This helps me to see that the ingredients are well distributed. Leavenings, such as yeast, baking powder, and baking soda, have a short shelf life. I recommend making your bread mixes within the week that you will be giving them away, and putting a two-month expiration date on your gift tag instructions. Store bread mixes in airtight florist's cellophane, plastic bags, or canisters.

Bread mixes present a variety of choices for packaging. They can be put into baskets with soup mix and a dessert mix to make a "meal basket." When giving bread mixes, include a flavored butter or jar of jam. Line the bread basket with a pretty linen dish towel and include a spreading knife for the jam. Bread mixes can be given with a breadboard and a serrated knife, and outer-wrapped in layers of colored tissue paper, tied with coordinating ribbon. When giving a bread mix, keep in mind the shape of the finished loaf. Use a long, narrow basket for French bread, and a smaller, round basket for California Corn Bread (see page 68). French Baguette Mix (see page 71) can be given with a baguette pan for baking. Eucalyptus Stoneware (see Source Guide) has my favorite baskets for giving breads. These ceramic baskets can be put into a hot oven to heat rolls or bread and will help to keep the rolls warm during a meal. A bread mix can also be given by itself as a hostess gift with the recipe attached.

Beer Bread Mix

Makes 1 loaf

T his is the recipe that gave me the idea for this book. As you can see, this recipe has many variations, and I have included just a few. Although the beer gives the bread a nice yeasty flavor, your friends may want to substitute a 12-ounce bottle of unflavored seltzer. Pack the bread mix in an airtight container or bag, and give it in a bread pan lined with a cloth napkin. The Dilly Beer Bread can be given along with a small dill plant in the basket. A large beer stein with hinged lid would make an unexpected, whimsical container.

3 cups self-rising flour   **3 tablespoons sugar**

In a large mixing bowl, combine the ingredients. Whisk together until the sugar is distributed in the flour. Place the mix in an airtight jar or plastic bag.

Beer Bread
Makes 1 loaf

1 package Beer Bread
  Mix
1 12-ounce can beer or
  1 12-ounce bottle
  unflavored seltzer

½ cup butter, melted

Preheat the oven to 375°F. In a large mixing bowl, combine the Beer Bread Mix with the beer or seltzer, beating the mixture with a wooden spoon. The batter will be lumpy. Place the batter into a greased loaf pan. Pour ⅓ of the butter over the dough. Bake for 40 minutes, then pour ⅓ of the butter over the top of the bread. Continue baking for 10 minutes more. Pour the last ⅓ of the butter onto the bread and bake 10 minutes longer. Remove the bread from the oven. Allow to cool for 30 to 40 minutes, and serve warm.

Dilly Beer Bread

Follow same ingredients list as for Beer Bread, but add 2 tablespoons dried dillweed, or ¼ cup fresh snipped dill. Amend directions to include dill in blend. All other recipe steps are the same.

Cheesy Beer Bread

Follow same ingredients list as for Beer Bread, but add 1 cup grated Cheddar cheese or Swiss cheese, and 4 shakes hot pepper sauce. Amend directions to include cheese and pepper in blend. All other recipe steps are the same.

Whole Wheat Beer Bread Mix

Makes 1 loaf

Whole Wheat Beer Bread Mix would be lovely presented in a basket lined with a napkin, accompanied by a small jar of honey and a wooden honey server.

2½ cups self-rising flour　　**3 tablespoons sugar**
½ cup whole wheat flour

In a large mixing bowl, combine the ingredients with a wire whisk. Place the mix in an airtight container.

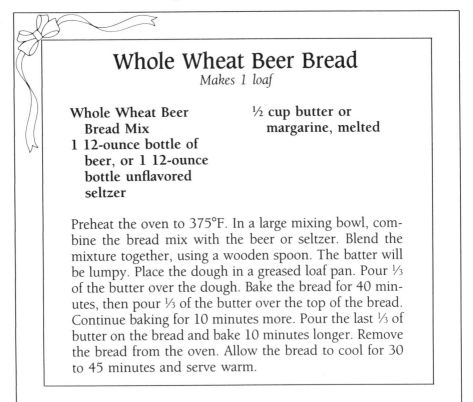

Whole Wheat Beer Bread
Makes 1 loaf

Whole Wheat Beer　　**½ cup butter or**
Bread Mix　　　　　**margarine, melted**
1 12-ounce bottle of
beer, or 1 12-ounce
bottle unflavored
seltzer

Preheat the oven to 375°F. In a large mixing bowl, combine the bread mix with the beer or seltzer. Blend the mixture together, using a wooden spoon. The batter will be lumpy. Place the dough in a greased loaf pan. Pour ⅓ of the butter over the dough. Bake the bread for 40 minutes, then pour ⅓ of the butter over the top of the bread. Continue baking for 10 minutes more. Pour the last ⅓ of butter on the bread and bake 10 minutes longer. Remove the bread from the oven. Allow the bread to cool for 30 to 45 minutes and serve warm.

Muffin Mix

Makes 1 dozen muffins

T his basic mix can be given by itself with a recipe card for the different variations, or it can be tucked into a white lidded basket with some mugs and beverage mixes (see pages 109–124). When they are in season, include fresh blueberries or raspberries in the basket for those muffin mix variations.

2 cups self-rising flour
½ cup sugar
¼ cup brown sugar

1 teaspoon cinnamon
¼ teaspoon nutmeg

Combine all the ingredients in a large mixing bowl. Blend together with a wire whisk. Place the mix into an airtight container.

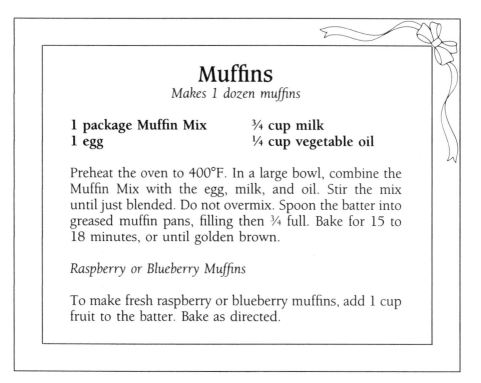

Muffins
Makes 1 dozen muffins

1 package Muffin Mix
1 egg

¾ cup milk
¼ cup vegetable oil

Preheat the oven to 400°F. In a large bowl, combine the Muffin Mix with the egg, milk, and oil. Stir the mix until just blended. Do not overmix. Spoon the batter into greased muffin pans, filling then ¾ full. Bake for 15 to 18 minutes, or until golden brown.

Raspberry or Blueberry Muffins

To make fresh raspberry or blueberry muffins, add 1 cup fruit to the batter. Bake as directed.

Apple Muffin Mix

Makes 1 dozen muffins

A great morning starter. Tuck this mix into a wooden apple basket lined with a coordinating napkin. Dried apples can usually be found in airtight pouches near the raisins in the supermarket.

2 cups self-rising flour
½ cup sugar
¼ cup brown sugar

1 teaspoon cinnamon
¼ teaspoon nutmeg
1 cup chopped dried apple

In a large mixing bowl, combine all the ingredients. Place the mix into an airtight container.

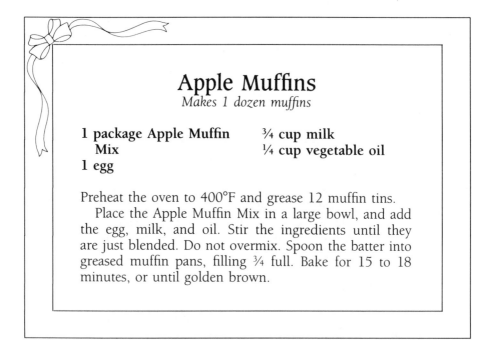

Apple Muffins

Makes 1 dozen muffins

1 package Apple Muffin Mix
1 egg

¾ cup milk
¼ cup vegetable oil

Preheat the oven to 400°F and grease 12 muffin tins.

Place the Apple Muffin Mix in a large bowl, and add the egg, milk, and oil. Stir the ingredients until they are just blended. Do not overmix. Spoon the batter into greased muffin pans, filling ¾ full. Bake for 15 to 18 minutes, or until golden brown.

Date and Nut Muffin Mix

Makes 1 dozen muffins

Give this variation from the Basic Muffin Mix in a Eucalyptus Stoneware (see Source Guide) muffin basket with a package of dates and freshly ground vanilla nut coffee.

2 cups self-rising flour	**1 teaspoon cinnamon**
½ cup sugar	**¼ teaspoon nutmeg**
¼ cup brown sugar	**½ cup chopped pecans**

In a medium bowl, combine all the ingredients, and blend with a wire whisk. Place the mix into an airtight container.

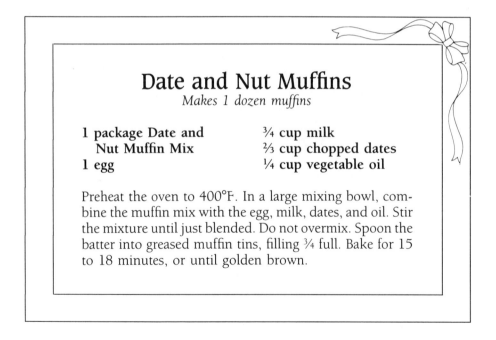

Date and Nut Muffins
Makes 1 dozen muffins

1 package Date and Nut Muffin Mix	**¾ cup milk**
	⅔ cup chopped dates
1 egg	**¼ cup vegetable oil**

Preheat the oven to 400°F. In a large mixing bowl, combine the muffin mix with the egg, milk, dates, and oil. Stir the mixture until just blended. Do not overmix. Spoon the batter into greased muffin tins, filling ¾ full. Bake for 15 to 18 minutes, or until golden brown.

Ginger Spice Muffin Mix

Makes 1 dozen muffins

A t Christmastime, give Ginger Spice Muffin Mix packed in airtight decorative jars. Cover jar tops with Christmas fabric, and tie red and green ribbon around the lids. Attach gift tag instructions to the ribbon.

1¾ cups all-purpose flour
2 tablespoons sugar
2 tablespoons brown sugar
3 teaspoons baking powder
½ teaspoon baking soda
½ teaspoon salt

1 teaspoon ground
  cinnamon
½ teaspoon ground nutmeg
¼ teaspoon ground ginger
¼ teaspoon ground cloves

Combine all the ingredients in a medium bowl. Store the mixture in an airtight container.

Ginger Spice Muffins

Makes 1 dozen muffins

1 package Ginger Spice
  Muffin Mix
¼ cup butter or
  margarine, melted

1 egg
1 teaspoon vanilla
1 cup milk

Preheat the oven to 400°F, and grease 12 muffin tins. In a large bowl, combine the muffin mix with the butter, egg, vanilla, and milk. Stir the mixture until the ingredients are blended. Do not overmix. The batter will be lumpy. Fill muffin tins ⅔ full, and bake for 15 minutes.

Bran Muffin Mix

Makes 1 dozen muffins

B ran muffins are a great wake-up call. I like to give this mix as a hostess gift with a ceramic heart-shaped muffin pan.

1½ cups All-Bran Cereal	**½ cup sugar**
1¼ cups self-rising flour	**1 cup golden raisins**

In a large mixing bowl, combine all the ingredients, Store the mixture in an airtight container.

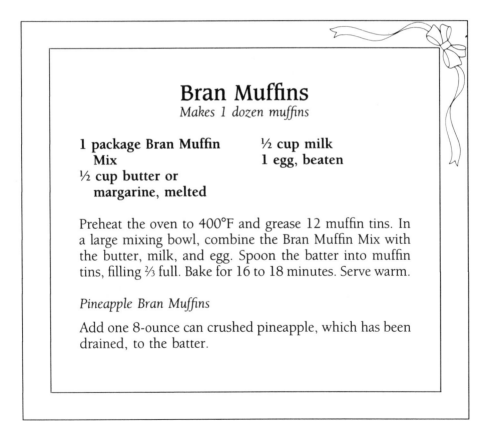

Bran Muffins

Makes 1 dozen muffins

1 package Bran Muffin Mix	**½ cup milk**
½ cup butter or margarine, melted	**1 egg, beaten**

Preheat the oven to 400°F and grease 12 muffin tins. In a large mixing bowl, combine the Bran Muffin Mix with the butter, milk, and egg. Spoon the batter into muffin tins, filling ⅔ full. Bake for 16 to 18 minutes. Serve warm.

Pineapple Bran Muffins

Add one 8-ounce can crushed pineapple, which has been drained, to the batter.

California Corn Bread Mix

Makes 3 cups

T his is a sweet, cakelike corn bread that is delicious with honey butter or strawberry butter. Give California Corn Bread Mix in an 8-inch cast-iron skillet, with a small serrated bread knife. Add a "country" gift wrap: a red-and-white bandanna-print dish towel or large dinner napkin.

2 cups Bisquick baking mix
½ cup cornmeal
½ cup sugar

1 tablespoon baking powder

In a large glass or ceramic mixing bowl, stir all the ingredients together. Store the mix in an airtight container.

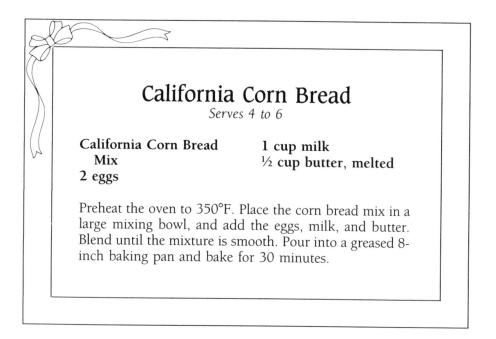

California Corn Bread

Serves 4 to 6

California Corn Bread Mix
2 eggs

1 cup milk
½ cup butter, melted

Preheat the oven to 350°F. Place the corn bread mix in a large mixing bowl, and add the eggs, milk, and butter. Blend until the mixture is smooth. Pour into a greased 8-inch baking pan and bake for 30 minutes.

Mom's Heirloom Brown Bread Mix

Makes 4½ cups

T his is a very old recipe, a delicious addition to anyone's bread collection. Mom's Heirloom Brown Bread Mix makes a nice housewarming gift tucked into a basket with some coffee mugs filled with flavored coffees or teas (see Beverage Mixes).

2 cups whole wheat flour	**1 cup chopped dates**
½ cup all-purpose flour	**1 teaspoon salt**
2 teaspoons baking soda	**1 cup raisins**

In a medium bowl, combine the ingredients, and stir until well blended. Store the mix in an airtight container.

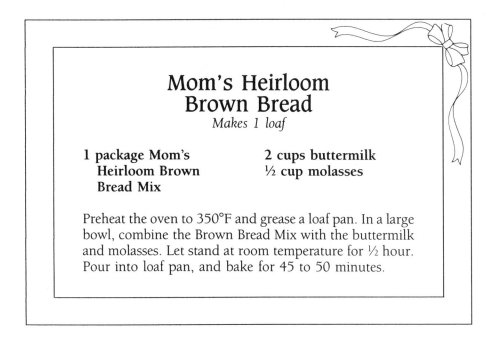

Mom's Heirloom Brown Bread
Makes 1 loaf

1 package Mom's Heirloom Brown Bread Mix

2 cups buttermilk
½ cup molasses

Preheat the oven to 350°F and grease a loaf pan. In a large bowl, combine the Brown Bread Mix with the buttermilk and molasses. Let stand at room temperature for ½ hour. Pour into loaf pan, and bake for 45 to 50 minutes.

Irish Soda Bread Mix

Makes 5 cups

T his bit of Ireland makes a welcome treat on a Sunday morning with a cup of Earl Grey or Irish Breakfast tea. Pack Irish Soda Bread Mix in a handled basket with assorted teas and mugs. Extend the theme by including a set of napkins in kelly green and white to line the basket, then decorate with green and white ribbons.

2½ cups all-purpose flour
½ cup whole wheat flour
1 cup dried currants
1 cup light-brown sugar

1 tablespoon baking powder
1 teaspoon baking soda

In a medium mixing bowl, combine all the ingredients. Store the mix in an airtight container.

Irish Soda Bread

Makes 1 loaf

1 package Irish Soda Bread Mix
¼ cup butter or margarine, softened

2 eggs
1½ cups buttermilk

Preheat the oven to 350°F and grease and flour a 9-inch springform pan. Place the Irish Soda Bread Mix in a large bowl. Cut the butter into the mix. Add the eggs and buttermilk, and stir to blend. When the mixture is smooth, pour into the greased and floured pan. Bake the bread for 45 minutes, or until a toothpick inserted into the middle comes out clean. Serve warm.

French Baguette Mix

Makes 4½ cups

Baguettes are long loaves of French bread. Give the mix with a double baguette pan to bake it in, or line a long basket with napkins, one each red, white, and blue, then place the pan and mix in the basket, with a Maurice Chevalier tape and a gift certificate to a local cheese shop. Wrap the basket in tricolor tissue papers and ribbons.

4 cups bread flour
½ cup whole wheat flour
3 packages dry active yeast

Pinch of sugar
1½ teaspoons salt

In a large bowl, combine all the ingredients. Store the mix in an airtight container.

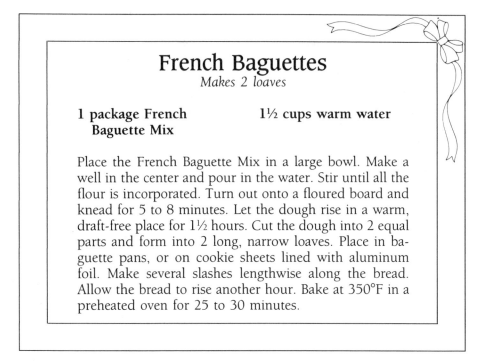

French Baguettes

Makes 2 loaves

1 package French
Baguette Mix

1½ cups warm water

Place the French Baguette Mix in a large bowl. Make a well in the center and pour in the water. Stir until all the flour is incorporated. Turn out onto a floured board and knead for 5 to 8 minutes. Let the dough rise in a warm, draft-free place for 1½ hours. Cut the dough into 2 equal parts and form into 2 long, narrow loaves. Place in baguette pans, or on cookie sheets lined with aluminum foil. Make several slashes lengthwise along the bread. Allow the bread to rise another hour. Bake at 350°F in a preheated oven for 25 to 30 minutes.

Honey Whole Wheat Bread Mix

Makes 5⅓ cups

W hole wheat bread is a welcome smell on a cold winter evening, or any time! Place the bread mix in an airtight cellophane bag. Tie it to a long breadboard, with a serrated bread knife and a jar of honey. Wrap the gift in colored cellophane and tie with grosgrain ribbon. You can also team this mix with the World's Best Bean Soup Mix (see page 28) in a picnic basket lined with a checkered tablecloth.

4¾ cups whole wheat flour
2 packages dry active yeast

1 tablespoon salt
2 tablespoons brown sugar
½ cup all-purpose flour

In a large mixing bowl, combine all the ingredients. Place the mix into an airtight container.

Honey Whole Wheat Bread

Makes 2 loaves

1 package Honey
   Whole Wheat Bread
   Mix
2 cups warm milk
¼ cup butter or
   margarine, melted

½ cup honey
1 cup all-purpose flour
   (as needed)
2 tablespoons butter,
   melted

Preheat the oven to 375°F, and grease 2 loaf pans. Place the Honey Whole Wheat Bread Mix into a large bowl and make a well in the center. Add the milk, butter, and honey, stirring with a wooden spoon until all ingredients are combined and smooth. Turn out onto a floured board and knead the dough, adding up to 1 cup of all-purpose flour. Place the dough in a greased bowl, cover, and let rise for 1 hour, or until doubled in bulk. Punch down the dough, and let rise another 45 minutes. Cut the dough in half and shape into 2 loaves. Place in greased loaf pans, cover, and let rise 45 minutes. Bake the bread for 30 to 40 minutes. At the end of the baking time, brush the loaves with melted butter.

Indian Squaw Bread Mix

Makes 12½ cups

T his delicious bread, well known in Southern California, is almost like cake, but robust enough for the best of sandwiches. Give Indian Squaw Bread Mix in a woven Indian basket with a coordinating napkin to line the bottom. Add jam and a serrated knife.

1 tablespoon dry yeast
1 tablespoon salt
½ cup dark-brown sugar

4 cups whole wheat flour
8 cups all-purpose flour

Combine the ingredients into a glass bowl. Store in an airtight container.

Indian Squaw Bread

Makes 2 round loaves

1 package Indian
   Squaw Bread Mix
¾ cup unsulfured dark
   molasses
1¼ cups vegetable oil

3 cups lukewarm water
All-purpose flour
   (as needed)

Place the Indian Squaw Bread Mix in a glass or ceramic mixing bowl. Add the molasses, oil, and water and beat with a dough hook or wooden spoon until the dough holds together. Turn the dough out onto a floured board, and knead in enough all-purpose flour to form a smooth elastic dough. Transfer the dough to an oiled bowl, turning the dough to coat it with the oil. Let the dough rise, covered, in a warm place for 3 to 4 hours, or until it has tripled in bulk. Punch the dough down, and divide it into two halves. Form each loaf into 12-inch rounds. Arrange the loaves on a buttered baking sheet. Let the dough rise again for 30 to 40 minutes, or until it has doubled.

Preheat the oven to 300°F. Bake the loaves for 1 hour and 10 minutes. They will sound hollow when the bottom is tapped. Transfer the loaves to a rack and let them cool.

Scone Mix

Makes 2⅛ cups

S cones make an elegant gift. Give Scone Mix in a handled basket with a selection of teas and a jam of your choice. Or, you can make this into a "breakfast-in-bed basket." Fill a matching sugar bowl and creamer with Scone Mix and seal with cling plastic wrap. Tuck a selection of teas and a jar of jam into a small basket, and place it on a breakfast tray with the sugar bowl and creamer, plus two small plates, and a pair of matching teacups and saucers. Include a small plant, or a rose in a bud vase and a book of poetry.

2 cups all-purpose flour
1 teaspoon baking soda
1 teaspoon salt

2 teaspoons cream of tartar

Combine all the ingredients in a medium mixing bowl. Place the mix in an airtight container.

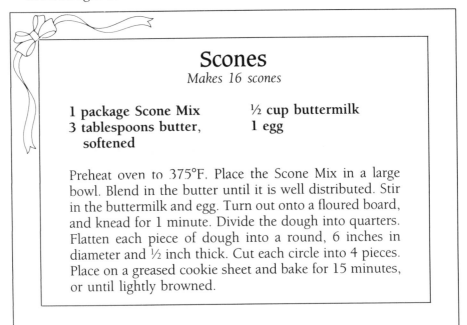

Scones
Makes 16 scones

1 package Scone Mix
3 tablespoons butter, softened

½ cup buttermilk
1 egg

Preheat oven to 375°F. Place the Scone Mix in a large bowl. Blend in the butter until it is well distributed. Stir in the buttermilk and egg. Turn out onto a floured board, and knead for 1 minute. Divide the dough into quarters. Flatten each piece of dough into a round, 6 inches in diameter and ½ inch thick. Cut each circle into 4 pieces. Place on a greased cookie sheet and bake for 15 minutes, or until lightly browned.

Pizza, Pancake, Popover, and Doughnut Mixes

A variation on the bread mix theme, these mixes will provide enjoyment and delicious rewards. The pizza mix is a natural for a basket filled with Italian goodies: homemade sauce, cheeses, olive oil, Biscotti Mix (see page 100), and a pizza pan. The pancakes make a wonderful presentation in a breakfast basket with syrups, jams, and breakfast beverage mixes. Popovers are such a special treat, your friends will love the introduction to this savory mix. And doughnuts are a whimsical gift that could be given to a family new to the neighborhood with mugs for coffee or drink mixes.

Consistent with preparing the other bread mixes, be sure to make these mixes within the week that you wish to give them; label with a two-month expiration date, and store in airtight containers.

Additional gift accessories and packaging tips will be found with individual recipes that follow.

Dutch Baby Pancake Mix

Makes 1¼ cups

"Dutch Babies" are oven-baked pancakes that rise to glorious heights in a very hot oven. Give this mix in a basket with a jug of pure maple syrup, or with fresh strawberries and a small shaker jar of confectioners' sugar.

1 cup all-purpose flour   ¼ cup sugar
1 teaspoon ground
   cinnamon

In a medium mixing bowl, combine all the ingredients. Store the mix in an airtight container.

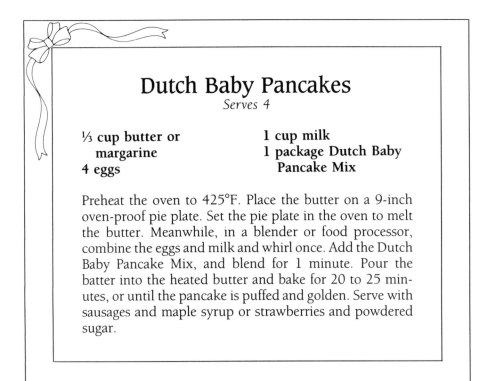

Dutch Baby Pancakes
Serves 4

⅓ cup butter or   1 cup milk
   margarine   1 package Dutch Baby
4 eggs   Pancake Mix

Preheat the oven to 425°F. Place the butter on a 9-inch oven-proof pie plate. Set the pie plate in the oven to melt the butter. Meanwhile, in a blender or food processor, combine the eggs and milk and whirl once. Add the Dutch Baby Pancake Mix, and blend for 1 minute. Pour the batter into the heated butter and bake for 20 to 25 minutes, or until the pancake is puffed and golden. Serve with sausages and maple syrup or strawberries and powdered sugar.

Connemara Pancake Mix

Makes 2⅔ cups

Hearty and nutritious, these pancakes from the area in Ireland called Connemara can be packed into a hostess basket with maple syrup, Canadian bacon, and fresh oranges for juice. Spread a lovely Irish linen kitchen towel over the basket.

1¼ cups all-purpose flour
½ cup whole wheat flour
⅔ cup sugar
¼ cup Irish oats
1 tablespoon sunflower
  seeds

1 tablespoon sesame
  seeds
2 teaspoons baking
  powder
¼ teaspoon cinnamon

In a medium bowl, blend the ingredients together with a wire whisk. Store in an airtight container.

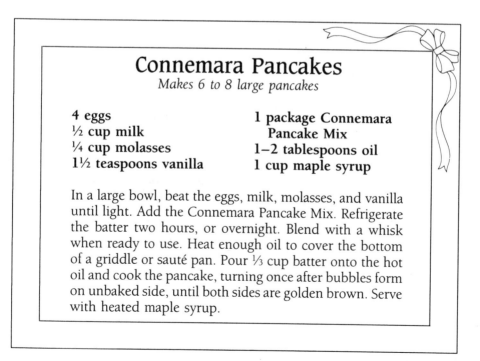

Connemara Pancakes

Makes 6 to 8 large pancakes

4 eggs
½ cup milk
¼ cup molasses
1½ teaspoons vanilla

1 package Connemara
  Pancake Mix
1–2 tablespoons oil
1 cup maple syrup

In a large bowl, beat the eggs, milk, molasses, and vanilla until light. Add the Connemara Pancake Mix. Refrigerate the batter two hours, or overnight. Blend with a whisk when ready to use. Heat enough oil to cover the bottom of a griddle or sauté pan. Pour ⅓ cup batter onto the hot oil and cook the pancake, turning once after bubbles form on unbaked side, until both sides are golden brown. Serve with heated maple syrup.

Herbed Popover Mix

Makes 2⅛ cups

Popovers are fun to make and can be made in popover pans or glass custard cups. Give someone this mix with a popover pan and they will be delighted. Custard cups can be filled with Herbed Popover Mix, sealed with cling plastic wrap, then topped with ribbon rosettes of different colors.

2 cups all-purpose flour
1 teaspoon salt

¼ teaspoon dried thyme
¼ teaspoon crumbled sage

In a medium mixing bowl, combine all the ingredients, and stir with a wire whisk until the spices are well distributed throughout. Store the mix in an airtight container

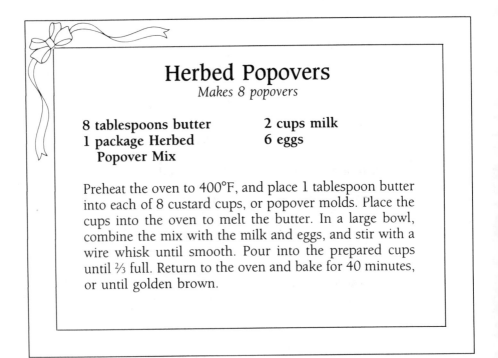

Herbed Popovers

Makes 8 popovers

8 tablespoons butter
1 package Herbed Popover Mix

2 cups milk
6 eggs

Preheat the oven to 400°F, and place 1 tablespoon butter into each of 8 custard cups, or popover molds. Place the cups into the oven to melt the butter. In a large bowl, combine the mix with the milk and eggs, and stir with a wire whisk until smooth. Pour into the prepared cups until ⅔ full. Return to the oven and bake for 40 minutes, or until golden brown.

Oatmeal Doughnut Drop Mix

Makes 1½ cups

F or a new neighbor, pack this doughnut mix in a basket filled
with several kinds of teas, a shaker of cinnamon sugar, a street
map of the area, and a list of your favorite stores and merchants.

⅓ cup brown sugar
1 teaspoon salt
¾ cup flour
1 tablespoon dry yeast

1 teaspoon cinnamon
1 cup all-purpose flour
½ cup quick rolled oats

In a large mixing bowl, combine all the ingredients. Place the mix in
an airtight container.

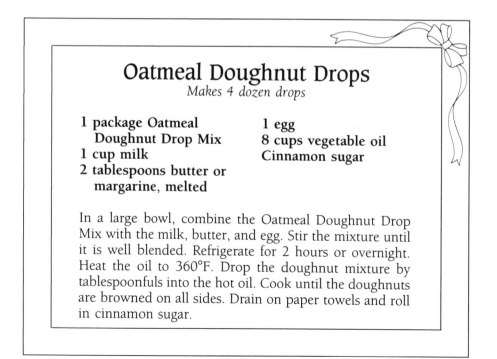

Oatmeal Doughnut Drops
Makes 4 dozen drops

1 package Oatmeal
  Doughnut Drop Mix
1 cup milk
2 tablespoons butter or
  margarine, melted

1 egg
8 cups vegetable oil
Cinnamon sugar

In a large bowl, combine the Oatmeal Doughnut Drop
Mix with the milk, butter, and egg. Stir the mixture until
it is well blended. Refrigerate for 2 hours or overnight.
Heat the oil to 360°F. Drop the doughnut mixture by
tablespoonfuls into the hot oil. Cook until the doughnuts
are browned on all sides. Drain on paper towels and roll
in cinnamon sugar.

Hot Cross Bun Mix

Makes 6¼ cups

T raditionally, hot cross buns were made on Good Friday, and were believed to have healing powers. These buns are a delightful addition to any pantry. Pack Hot Cross Bun Mix in clear glass jars with the recipe attached to streamer ribbons tied at the top.

4½ cups all-purpose flour
½ cup sugar
1 teaspoon cinnamon
¼ teaspoon nutmeg
⅛ teaspoon ground cloves

1 package active dry yeast
1 cup currants or raisins
1 teaspoon dried lemon
  peel

In a large mixing bowl, combine all the ingredients. Store the mix in an airtight container.

Hot Cross Buns
Makes 18 buns

1 cup milk
¼ cup butter or
  margarine
1 package Hot Cross
  Bun Mix
2 eggs

Frosting
1 cup powdered
  sugar
1 teaspoon lemon
  juice
½ teaspoon vanilla

In a small saucepan, heat the milk and butter until warm (110°F). Place the Hot Cross Bun Mix in a large bowl, and make a well in the center. Add the milk mixture and beat until the dough is soft. Add the eggs, and beat until the dough is smooth. Turn the dough out onto a floured board, and knead until the dough is elastic. Place in an oiled bowl and cover with plastic wrap. Allow the dough to rise in a warm place until doubled in bulk, about 1 hour.

Punch the dough down, and divide into 18 equal pieces, forming each into a ball. Place in a greased 13- by 9-inch pan. Cover and allow to rise for about 1 hour.

Preheat the oven to 375°F, and cut a cross on top of each bun with a sharp knife or scissors. Bake for 20 to 25 minutes or until golden. Remove the buns from the pan and allow to cool.

Frosting: In a small bowl, combine the powdered sugar with the lemon juice and vanilla. When cool, form a cross on each bun with frosting.

Beignet Mix

Makes 1½ cups

B eignets are hot fritters that are traditionally served with a cup of dark, rich coffee for breakfast in New Orleans. Give this mix in a linen-lined basket with a pound of French roast coffee, some mugs, and a shaker filled with confectioners' sugar.

1 cup all-purpose flour
½ cup sugar
¼ teaspoon cinnamon

⅛ teaspoon nutmeg
¼ teaspoon salt

In a medium mixing bowl, combine all the ingredients. Store the mix in an airtight container.

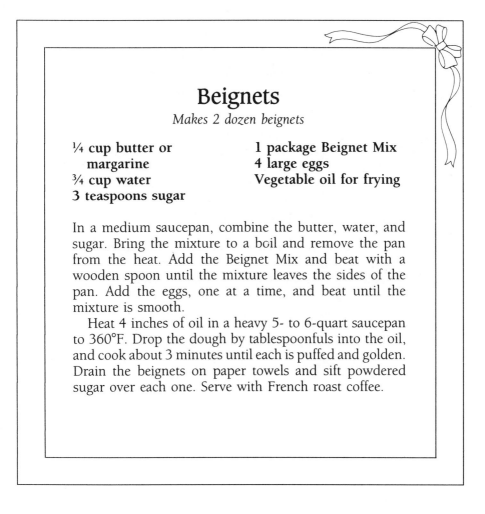

Beignets

Makes 2 dozen beignets

¼ cup butter or
  margarine
¾ cup water
3 teaspoons sugar

1 package Beignet Mix
4 large eggs
Vegetable oil for frying

In a medium saucepan, combine the butter, water, and sugar. Bring the mixture to a boil and remove the pan from the heat. Add the Beignet Mix and beat with a wooden spoon until the mixture leaves the sides of the pan. Add the eggs, one at a time, and beat until the mixture is smooth.

Heat 4 inches of oil in a heavy 5- to 6-quart saucepan to 360°F. Drop the dough by tablespoonfuls into the oil, and cook about 3 minutes until each is puffed and golden. Drain the beignets on paper towels and sift powdered sugar over each one. Serve with French roast coffee.

Focaccia Mix

Makes one 13- by 9-inch bread

F ocaccia is a delicious Italian flatbread that is a delightful accompaniment to soups and appetizers. Focaccia Mix can be given
with Minestrone Soup Mix (see page 34) in a basket with a bottle of
red wine and a jar of Pesto (see page 134) to spread on the bread. Or
include this unusual bread mix in a basket with an assortment of other
bread mixes to create a bread sampler basket.

**1 package active dry yeast
1 tablespoon sugar
1½ teaspoons crushed red
  pepper flakes**

**1½ teaspoons dried
  rosemary
1½ cups bread flour
½ teaspoon salt**

Combine the ingredients in a glass bowl, and blend with a wire whisk.
Store the mix in an airtight container.

Focaccia
Serves 6

1 package Focaccia Mix	Salt
½ cup warm water	Pesto
4 tablespoons olive oil	

Place the Focaccia Mix in a large ceramic or glass mixing bowl. Add the warm water and 2 tablespoons of the olive oil. Blend the dough with a dough hook or wooden spoon until it is smooth. If it is dry, add water by the tablespoon. If it sticks, add a bit of flour. Turn the bread onto a floured board, and knead the bread until it is smooth. Transfer to an oiled bowl, and rotate the dough to coat the surface with oil. Cover with plastic wrap and let rise in a warm spot until doubled in bulk (approximately one hour).

Preheat the oven to 425°F. Punch the dough down onto a floured board. Roll the dough into a 13- by 9-inch rectangle. Place in an oiled 13- by 9-inch pan, and brush with the remaining olive oil. Sprinkle the surface with salt. Bake for 5 minutes. Use a fork to pierce air bubbles on the surface and continue to bake until golden brown, about 8 minutes more. Remove from the pan and cut into 3-inch squares. Serve warm with pesto.

Pizza Dough Mix

Makes 3 cups

T his is a gift for friends of all ages, whether a starving college student or a senior citizen; everyone loves pizza. Start off by making the pizza dough mix and then give it with a pizza pan, home-made pizza sauce, a bottle of virgin olive oil, and imported Parmesan and fresh mozzarella cheeses. Tie it up in a red-and-white checkered tablecloth and include some napkins. Another gift-giving suggestion: Tie the package of Pizza Dough Mix to the top of a wooden pizza peel, with a pizza cutter. Use red, white, and green streamer ribbons to emphasize the Italian theme.

2¾ cups bread flour　　　　**2 teaspoons salt**
1 package active dry yeast

In a medium bowl, combine all the ingredients. Place the mix in an airtight container.

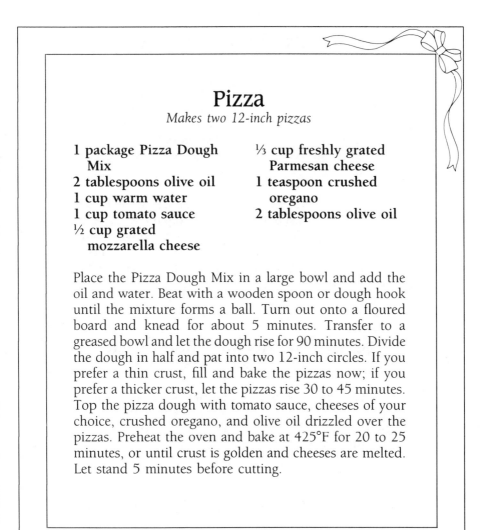

Pizza
Makes two 12-inch pizzas

1 package Pizza Dough
   Mix
2 tablespoons olive oil
1 cup warm water
1 cup tomato sauce
½ cup grated
   mozzarella cheese

⅓ cup freshly grated
   Parmesan cheese
1 teaspoon crushed
   oregano
2 tablespoons olive oil

Place the Pizza Dough Mix in a large bowl and add the oil and water. Beat with a wooden spoon or dough hook until the mixture forms a ball. Turn out onto a floured board and knead for about 5 minutes. Transfer to a greased bowl and let the dough rise for 90 minutes. Divide the dough in half and pat into two 12-inch circles. If you prefer a thin crust, fill and bake the pizzas now; if you prefer a thicker crust, let the pizzas rise 30 to 45 minutes. Top the pizza dough with tomato sauce, cheeses of your choice, crushed oregano, and olive oil drizzled over the pizzas. Preheat the oven and bake at 425°F for 20 to 25 minutes, or until crust is golden and cheeses are melted. Let stand 5 minutes before cutting.

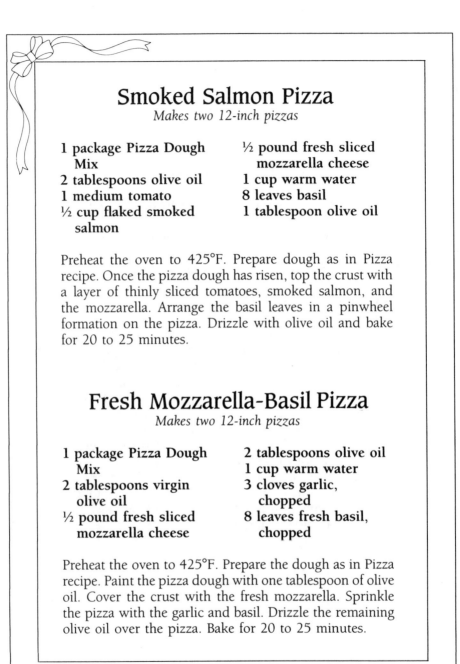

Smoked Salmon Pizza

Makes two 12-inch pizzas

1 package Pizza Dough
  Mix
2 tablespoons olive oil
1 medium tomato
½ cup flaked smoked
  salmon

½ pound fresh sliced
  mozzarella cheese
1 cup warm water
8 leaves basil
1 tablespoon olive oil

Preheat the oven to 425°F. Prepare dough as in Pizza recipe. Once the pizza dough has risen, top the crust with a layer of thinly sliced tomatoes, smoked salmon, and the mozzarella. Arrange the basil leaves in a pinwheel formation on the pizza. Drizzle with olive oil and bake for 20 to 25 minutes.

Fresh Mozzarella-Basil Pizza

Makes two 12-inch pizzas

1 package Pizza Dough
  Mix
2 tablespoons virgin
  olive oil
½ pound fresh sliced
  mozzarella cheese

2 tablespoons olive oil
1 cup warm water
3 cloves garlic,
  chopped
8 leaves fresh basil,
  chopped

Preheat the oven to 425°F. Prepare the dough as in Pizza recipe. Paint the pizza dough with one tablespoon of olive oil. Cover the crust with the fresh mozzarella. Sprinkle the pizza with the garlic and basil. Drizzle the remaining olive oil over the pizza. Bake for 20 to 25 minutes.

Cookie and Cake Mixes

Everyone loves an easy dessert, and the mixes in this chapter are guaranteed to delight your friends. Cookie and cake mixes are simple to prepare and take just a few ingredients added to the mix to create an easy snack or dessert.

During the holidays, a gift of a cookie mix can be just the right magic for a child when you include an apron, decorative sprinkles, and cookie cutters. A basket of assorted cake mixes can help provide inspiration in the kitchen for a friend.

Add a box of birthday-cake candles and tubes of colorful frostings to have on hand for special occasions. Give an assortment of individually bagged cookie mixes in a big cookie jar. Pretty party goods—decorated paper plates, matching napkins, and plastic forks—are all welcome accessories to accompany cake mix gifts.

When packaging dessert mixes, store them in airtight containers such as jars, canisters, florist's cellophane, or plastic bags.

Double-Fudge Brownie Mix

Makes 6 cups

D ense and fudgy, these are the best brownies in the world. I like to package this mix layered in a small glass canister with the instructions tied to a ribbon twisted around the top. Or fill a large measuring cup, seal it with cling plastic wrap twisted and closed around the handle, topped off by a ribbon rosette with curly ends.

2 cups sugar
1 cup cocoa (not Dutch
   process)

1 cup all-purpose flour
1 cup chopped pecans
1 cup chocolate chips

Mix all the ingredients together and store in an airtight container.

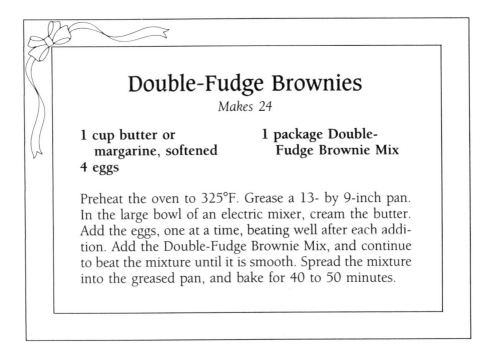

Double-Fudge Brownies

Makes 24

1 cup butter or
   margarine, softened
4 eggs

1 package Double-
   Fudge Brownie Mix

Preheat the oven to 325°F. Grease a 13- by 9-inch pan. In the large bowl of an electric mixer, cream the butter. Add the eggs, one at a time, beating well after each addition. Add the Double-Fudge Brownie Mix, and continue to beat the mixture until it is smooth. Spread the mixture into the greased pan, and bake for 40 to 50 minutes.

Molasses Cookie Mix

Makes 3¼ cups

S oft, crinkle-coated with sugar, and spicy, these old-fashioned cookies will delight your family and friends. Package the cookie mix in a cellophane bag and place it in a whimsical cookie jar to be filled later by recipients with the cookies they bake.

2 cups all-purpose flour
1 cup sugar
1 teaspoon baking soda
1 teaspoon baking powder
1 teaspoon ground ginger
1 teaspoon cinnamon

½ teaspoon ground nutmeg
¼ teaspoon ground cloves
⅛ teaspoon ground allspice

In a large mixing bowl, combine all the ingredients. Store the mix in an airtight container.

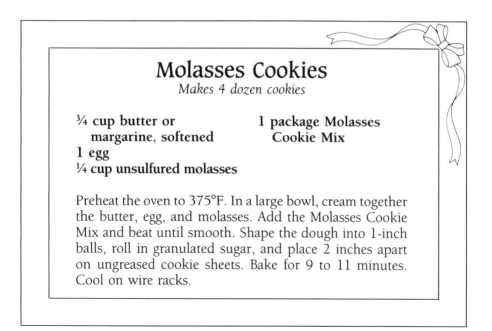

Molasses Cookies
Makes 4 dozen cookies

¾ cup butter or margarine, softened
1 egg
¼ cup unsulfured molasses

1 package Molasses Cookie Mix

Preheat the oven to 375°F. In a large bowl, cream together the butter, egg, and molasses. Add the Molasses Cookie Mix and beat until smooth. Shape the dough into 1-inch balls, roll in granulated sugar, and place 2 inches apart on ungreased cookie sheets. Bake for 9 to 11 minutes. Cool on wire racks.

Gingerbread Cookie Mix

Makes 3 cups

A simple and inexpensive gift, this mix can be packed in cellophane bags with unusual cookie cutters tied to a ribbon. Make small muslin bags with a drawstring to hold the package of cookie mix. Using fabric paints, stencil a gingerbread man to the front of the bag, and tie with ribbon. Attach a gingerbread-man cookie cutter and the gift tag instructions to the ribbon.

2½ cups all-purpose flour	¾ teaspoon ground ginger
¾ teaspoon salt	¼ teaspoon ground
½ cup sugar	nutmeg
½ teaspoon baking soda	

In a large mixing bowl, combine all the ingredients. Store in an airtight container.

Gingerbread Cookies

Makes about 3 dozen cookies

1 package Gingerbread Cookie Mix	½ cup butter or margarine, softened
½ cup molasses	¼ cup hot water

Preheat the oven to 375°F. Place the Gingerbread Cookie Mix in a large bowl, and add the molasses, butter, and water. Beat the mixture until it is smooth. Refrigerate the dough for 2 hours. Cut the dough into quarters and work with ¼ at a time. Roll the dough to ¼-inch thickness on a floured board. Cut into assorted shapes and place on ungreased cookie sheets. Bake for 8 to 9 minutes. Cool 2 minutes, then move to a rack to cool further. Repeat with remaining dough.

Oatmeal Cookie Mix

Makes 3⅔ cups

O atmeal cookies are just the thing for a housewarming gift. I like to pack this mix in a cellophane bag, placed in a lemonade crock or a sun-tea jar, which can then be used to serve cold drinks with a batch of fresh oatmeal cookies.

1 cup brown sugar	1 teaspoon baking soda
⅓ cup granulated sugar	1 teaspoon cinnamon
1½ cups all-purpose flour	3 cups quick rolled oats

In a large mixing bowl, combine all the ingredients with a wire whisk. Store the mix in an airtight container.

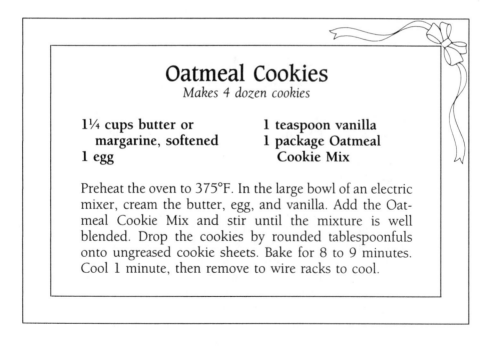

Oatmeal Cookies

Makes 4 dozen cookies

1¼ cups butter or margarine, softened	1 teaspoon vanilla
1 egg	1 package Oatmeal Cookie Mix

Preheat the oven to 375°F. In the large bowl of an electric mixer, cream the butter, egg, and vanilla. Add the Oatmeal Cookie Mix and stir until the mixture is well blended. Drop the cookies by rounded tablespoonfuls onto ungreased cookie sheets. Bake for 8 to 9 minutes. Cool 1 minute, then remove to wire racks to cool.

Snickerdoodle Mix

Makes 4¼ cups

S nickerdoodles are soft sugar cookies dusted with cinnamon sugar. Give this mix in a glass canister. Pack it into a white handled basket lined with a napkin, and include a chef's apron and hat, and a shaker of cinnamon sugar.

2¾ cups all-purpose flour
¼ teaspoon salt
1 teaspoon baking soda

2 teaspoons cream of tartar
1½ cups sugar

In a large mixing bowl, combine the ingredients, stirring with a wire whisk to blend. Store the mix in an airtight container.

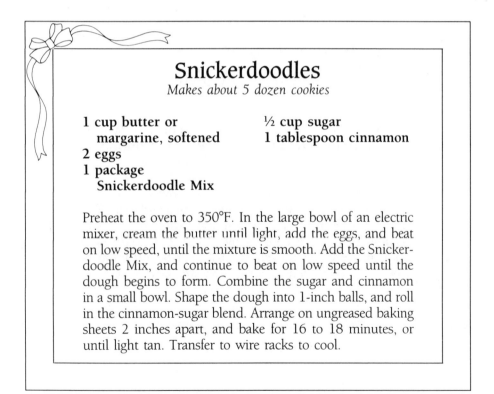

Snickerdoodles

Makes about 5 dozen cookies

1 cup butter or
   margarine, softened
2 eggs
1 package
   Snickerdoodle Mix

½ cup sugar
1 tablespoon cinnamon

Preheat the oven to 350°F. In the large bowl of an electric mixer, cream the butter until light, add the eggs, and beat on low speed, until the mixture is smooth. Add the Snickerdoodle Mix, and continue to beat on low speed until the dough begins to form. Combine the sugar and cinnamon in a small bowl. Shape the dough into 1-inch balls, and roll in the cinnamon-sugar blend. Arrange on ungreased baking sheets 2 inches apart, and bake for 16 to 18 minutes, or until light tan. Transfer to wire racks to cool.

Scottish Shortbread Mix

Makes 2¼ cups

T his old recipe never fails to bring a smile. Shortbread is a little bit of heaven. Give this mix with a shortbread mold. When not being used, the mold can be hung on the wall as a kitchen decoration. To give the package a Scottish flavor, wrap the mix with a Scotch-plaid ribbon.

1½ cups all-purpose flour   **¼ teaspoon salt**
¾ cup powdered sugar

In a medium mixing bowl, combine all the ingredients, blending well. Store the mix in an airtight container.

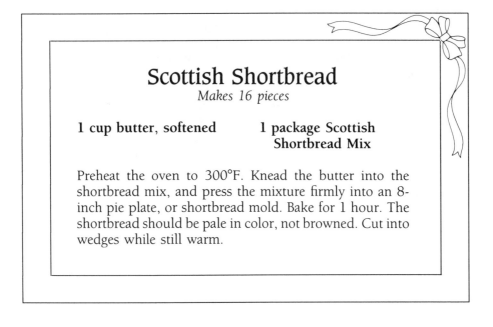

Scottish Shortbread
Makes 16 pieces

1 cup butter, softened   **1 package Scottish**
                                 Shortbread Mix

Preheat the oven to 300°F. Knead the butter into the shortbread mix, and press the mixture firmly into an 8-inch pie plate, or shortbread mold. Bake for 1 hour. The shortbread should be pale in color, not browned. Cut into wedges while still warm.

Old-Fashioned Pound Cake Mix

Makes 5¾ cups

T his pound cake is delicious all by itself, but becomes spectacular when paired with fresh strawberries or peaches. Give this summertime treat in a wooden basket with vanilla, orange, and lemon extracts, along with fresh fruits of the season. Old-Fashioned Pound Cake Mix also makes a nice addition to a cake sampler basket, when included with Chocolate Truffle Pound Cake Mix (see page 106) and Lemon Poppy-Seed Cake Mix (see page 102).

2¾ cups sugar　　　　　　1 teaspoon baking soda
3 cups flour

In a large glass bowl, combine the ingredients. Pack the mix in an airtight container.

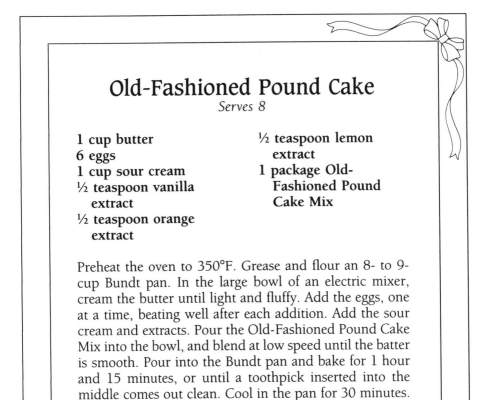

Old-Fashioned Pound Cake
Serves 8

1 cup butter
6 eggs
1 cup sour cream
½ teaspoon vanilla
   extract
½ teaspoon orange
   extract

½ teaspoon lemon
   extract
1 package Old-
   Fashioned Pound
   Cake Mix

Preheat the oven to 350°F. Grease and flour an 8- to 9-cup Bundt pan. In the large bowl of an electric mixer, cream the butter until light and fluffy. Add the eggs, one at a time, beating well after each addition. Add the sour cream and extracts. Pour the Old-Fashioned Pound Cake Mix into the bowl, and blend at low speed until the batter is smooth. Pour into the Bundt pan and bake for 1 hour and 15 minutes, or until a toothpick inserted into the middle comes out clean. Cool in the pan for 30 minutes. Unmold onto a wire rack, and cool completely.

Biscotti Mix

Makes 6¼ cups

T hese twice-baked Italian cookies are delightful when dipped into coffee or dessert wine. Give Biscotti Mix in a basket with a bottle of anise extract, Cappuccino Mix (see page 113), and a set of demitasse cups, saucers, and spoons. For an extra Italian accent, wrap in overlapping layers of red, white, and green tissue paper twisted together to make a big pompon on top.

2¾ cups all-purpose flour
2 cups chopped almonds
½ teaspoon baking powder
½ teaspoon baking soda
1½ cups sugar

¼ teaspoon dried lemon peel
¼ teaspoon dried orange peel

Combine all the ingredients in a large glass mixing bowl. Place the mix in an airtight container.

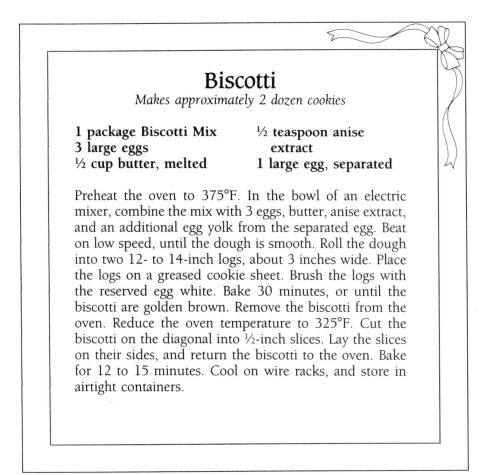

Biscotti

Makes approximately 2 dozen cookies

1 package Biscotti Mix
3 large eggs
½ cup butter, melted

½ teaspoon anise
extract
1 large egg, separated

Preheat the oven to 375°F. In the bowl of an electric mixer, combine the mix with 3 eggs, butter, anise extract, and an additional egg yolk from the separated egg. Beat on low speed, until the dough is smooth. Roll the dough into two 12- to 14-inch logs, about 3 inches wide. Place the logs on a greased cookie sheet. Brush the logs with the reserved egg white. Bake 30 minutes, or until the biscotti are golden brown. Remove the biscotti from the oven. Reduce the oven temperature to 325°F. Cut the biscotti on the diagonal into ½-inch slices. Lay the slices on their sides, and return the biscotti to the oven. Bake for 12 to 15 minutes. Cool on wire racks, and store in airtight containers.

Lemon Poppy-Seed Cake Mix

Makes 4¾ cups

T his pound cake is delightful with its sweet, tart, lemony flavor and the added crunch of poppy seeds. Give Lemon Poppy-Seed Cake Mix in a Bundt pan, add several fresh lemons, and group on a cake plate with an acrylic, high-domed lid, tied up with yellow streamer ribbons.

1½ cups sugar
3 cups cake flour
1½ teaspoons baking
  powder

¼ cup poppy seeds

Combine all the ingredients in a large mixing bowl. Blend with a wire whisk. Store the mix in an airtight container.

Lemon Poppy-Seed Cake

Serves 8

¾ cup butter
6 eggs
⅓ cup milk
1 teaspoon vanilla extract
1 teaspoon lemon extract
Zest of 1 lemon
1 package Lemon Poppy-
   Seed Cake Mix

Glaze
½ cup sugar
½ cup lemon juice

Preheat the oven to 350°F. Butter an 8- to 9-cup Bundt pan. In the large bowl of an electric mixer, cream the butter. Add the eggs, one at a time, beating after each addition. Add the milk, extracts, and lemon zest. The mixture will look curdled. Add the Cake Mix, and continue to beat on medium speed for 3 to 4 minutes until the mixture is smooth. Pour the batter into the greased pan, and bake for 45 to 55 minutes. While the cake is baking make the Glaze.

Glaze: Combine the sugar and lemon juice in a small saucepan over medium heat and bring the mixture to a boil for 3 minutes. When the cake has been removed from the oven, poke the cake all over with a wooden skewer, and brush the glaze over the cake. Let the cake stand for 1 hour, and remove from the pan to cool on a wire rack. Wrap the cake when it is cooled.

Ghirardelli Chocolate Cake Mix

Makes 6 cups

T his mix makes an old-fashioned chocolate cake that is sure to please even the fussiest of chocoholics. Create a chocolate lover's fantasy by giving this mix in a basket with Double-Fudge Brownie Mix (see page 92), Chocolate Truffle Pound Cake Mix (see page 106), and Hot Chocolate Mix (see page 115). Or you could give this mix by itself, in a cellophane bag, tied to a cake server. Ghirardelli chocolate is ground chocolate, not a cocoa, and can be found in the baking section of the supermarket. If you cannot find it, order directly from the Ghirardelli company (see Source Guide). A quick gift idea is to give someone a box of Ghirardelli chocolate with the recipe for the cake attached.

3 cups all-purpose flour
2 cups sugar
1 cup Ghirardelli ground chocolate

2 teaspoons baking soda

In a large mixing bowl, combine all the ingredients with a wire whisk. Store the mix in an airtight container.

Ghirardelli
Chocolate Cake
Serves 8 to 10

1 package Ghirardelli
  Chocolate Cake Mix
1 cup vegetable oil
1 cup buttermilk
2 eggs
1 cup boiling water
1 teaspoon vanilla
  extract

Cream Cheese
* Frosting*
1 pound powdered
  sugar
1 3-ounce package of
  cream cheese
½ cup butter or
  margarine,
  softened
2 tablespoons milk
1 teaspoon vanilla

Preheat the oven to 350°F. Place the cake mix in a large bowl and add the oil, buttermilk, eggs, water, and extract. Blend on low speed for 3 minutes, or until the mixture is smooth. Pour the batter into a greased 13- by 9-inch pan, and bake for 30 to 40 minutes. Remove from the oven and let cake cool.

Cream Cheese Frosting: In the small bowl of an electric mixer, cream together the sugar, cream cheese, and butter. Gradually add the milk and vanilla and beat the mixture until it is smooth, and of a spreading consistency. Frost cooled cake.

Chocolate Truffle Pound Cake Mix

Makes 6½ cups

T his dense, chocolaty pound cake will make a great gift to your
favorite chocolate lover. Pack the mix in a split-ash open basket
with a tin of cocoa and a jar of hot fudge sauce to satisfy your friend's
cravings.

3 cups sugar
3 cups flour
½ teaspoon salt

1 teaspoon baking soda
½ cup cocoa

In a medium mixing bowl, combine the ingredients and stir with a wire
whisk. Store the mix in an airtight container.

Chocolate Truffle
Pound Cake
Serves 8

¾ cup butter or
  margarine
5 eggs
1 cup milk
1 teaspoon vanilla
  extract

1 package Chocolate
  Truffle Pound Cake
  Mix

Preheat the oven to 325°F. Butter an 8- to 9-cup Bundt pan. In the large bowl of an electric mixer, cream the butter until it is smooth. Add the eggs one at a time, beating after each addition. Add the milk and vanilla, and beat the mixture until it is thoroughly blended. Add the Chocolate Truffle Pound Cake Mix and continue to beat for 3 minutes until smooth. Pour into prepared Bundt pan, and bake for 1 hour and 5 minutes, or until a toothpick inserted into the middle comes out clean. Cool for 25 minutes in the pan. Remove from the pan and cool on a wire rack.

Gingerbread Cake Mix

Makes 2½ cups

P ack Gingerbread Cake Mix in a cellophane bag tied with streamer ribbons and give it in a 9-inch round ceramic baking dish, lined with a pretty napkin, or place in a basket with a jar of unsulfured molasses, a serrated knife, four mugs, and a pound of vanilla-nut coffee.

2½ cups all-purpose flour
½ teaspoon baking
  powder
1 teaspoon baking soda

2 teaspoons ground
  ginger
1 teaspoon ground
  cinnamon

In a medium glass or ceramic mixing bowl, combine all the ingredients. Store the mix in an airtight container.

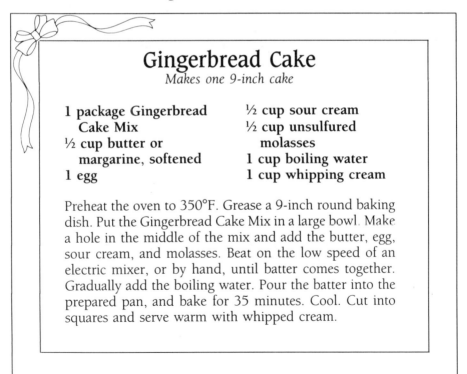

Gingerbread Cake
Makes one 9-inch cake

1 package Gingerbread
  Cake Mix
½ cup butter or
  margarine, softened
1 egg

½ cup sour cream
½ cup unsulfured
  molasses
1 cup boiling water
1 cup whipping cream

Preheat the oven to 350°F. Grease a 9-inch round baking dish. Put the Gingerbread Cake Mix in a large bowl. Make a hole in the middle of the mix and add the butter, egg, sour cream, and molasses. Beat on the low speed of an electric mixer, or by hand, until batter comes together. Gradually add the boiling water. Pour the batter into the prepared pan, and bake for 35 minutes. Cool. Cut into squares and serve warm with whipped cream.

Beverage Mixes

B everage mixes are a warm way to welcome a new neighbor, or they can be a small token of appreciation for a special friend. Packed into a unique mug, a beverage mix will be a reminder of your thoughtfulness long after the drink mix has been used. A snack or breakfast basket can include a variety of drink mixes with a cookie or quick bread mix. Spiced wine mixes can be tied to the neck of a bottle of dry red wine, and included in a basket with cheese and crackers.

Pack drink mixes in airtight containers, so the potency of the mixture is not diluted. Twist bags tightly before tying with ribbon, or use jars and containers with airtight lids. For added gift appeal, place a bag or two of tea mix in a charming Victorian teapot, wrap with layered colored tissue bunched at the lid, and tie with coordinating ribbon. For summertime giving, an outdoor acrylic ice bucket or pitcher makes a useful and appropriate container for packages of mixes that will be made into chilled drinks.

When making a coffee or tea drink, you have the option of choosing caffeinated or decaffeinated tea or coffee for each mix. Label your gift accordingly.

Mocha Coffee Mix

Makes 7 half-cup containers

A comforting gift for a friend or coworker, Mocha Coffee Mix is wonderful presented in a basket with a coffee thermos, some mugs, and a bar of imported chocolate.

¾ cup powdered nondairy
   creamer
1 cup sugar
¾ cup instant coffee
   (decaffeinated or
   regular)

6 tablespoons cocoa

Blend all the ingredients in a medium bowl. Store in an airtight container.

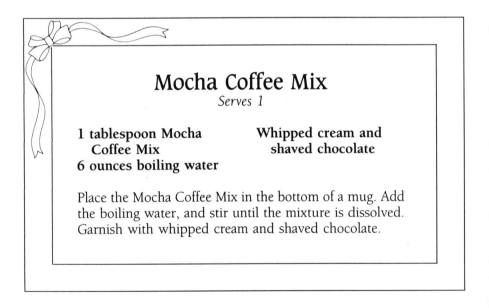

Mocha Coffee Mix

Serves 1

1 tablespoon Mocha
   Coffee Mix
6 ounces boiling water

Whipped cream and
   shaved chocolate

Place the Mocha Coffee Mix in the bottom of a mug. Add the boiling water, and stir until the mixture is dissolved. Garnish with whipped cream and shaved chocolate.

Chocolate Mint Coffee Mix

Makes 3 cups

Here's a great family gift to give at holiday time. Carefully choose a different mug for each family member, and pack coffee mix into each one. Decorate the mugs with candy canes and streamer ribbons.

¾ cup nondairy powdered
   creamer
1 cup sugar
¾ cup instant coffee
   (decaffeinated or
   regular)

¼ cup cocoa powder
6 hard peppermint
   candies broken into
   several pieces

Place all the ingredients into a blender or food processor, and process until the candies are pulverized. Store in airtight containers.

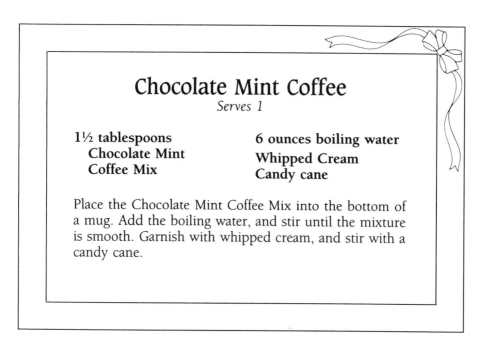

Chocolate Mint Coffee
Serves 1

1½ tablespoons
   Chocolate Mint
   Coffee Mix

6 ounces boiling water
Whipped Cream
Candy cane

Place the Chocolate Mint Coffee Mix into the bottom of a mug. Add the boiling water, and stir until the mixture is smooth. Garnish with whipped cream, and stir with a candy cane.

Coffee Continental Mix

Makes 1¾ cups

H ere's an easy gift for office coworkers or bridge group members at Christmastime. Give this mix in a mug, sealed and wrapped in cling plastic, with some party (colored) sugar—available from Select Origins (see Source Guide) in another little pack tied to the mug handle.

1 cup cocoa mix

¾ cup instant coffee (decaffeinated or regular)

Combine the ingredients in a bowl, and store in an airtight container.

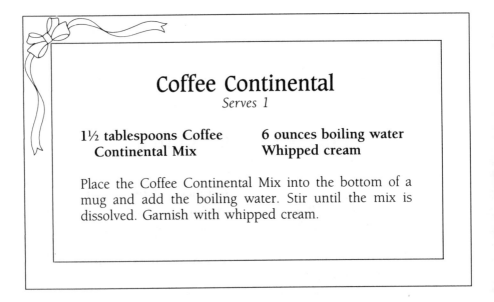

Coffee Continental

Serves 1

1½ tablespoons Coffee Continental Mix

6 ounces boiling water
Whipped cream

Place the Coffee Continental Mix into the bottom of a mug and add the boiling water. Stir until the mix is dissolved. Garnish with whipped cream.

Cappuccino Mix

Makes 3½ cups

P ack this delicious drink mix into a canister, and tuck it into a basket with a 2-ounce bottle of Frangelico liqueur, cappuccino cups, demitasse spoons, and a bar of imported chocolate to shave over the top of each cup.

1 cup powdered instant
   nondairy creamer
1 cup chocolate-flavored
   drink mix
¾ cup instant coffee
   (decaffeinated or
   regular)

½ cup sugar
½ teaspoon ground
   cinnamon
¼ teaspoon ground
   nutmeg

Combine all the ingredients in a medium bowl. Store in an airtight container.

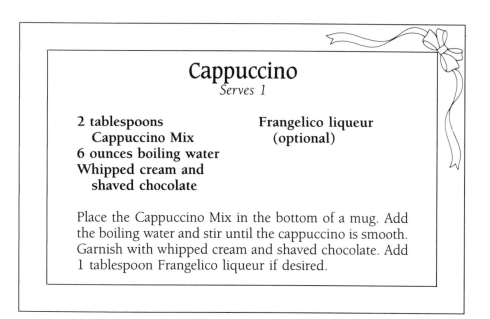

Cappuccino

Serves 1

2 tablespoons
   Cappuccino Mix
6 ounces boiling water
Whipped cream and
   shaved chocolate

Frangelico liqueur
   (optional)

Place the Cappuccino Mix in the bottom of a mug. Add the boiling water and stir until the cappuccino is smooth. Garnish with whipped cream and shaved chocolate. Add 1 tablespoon Frangelico liqueur if desired.

Spiced Mocha Coffee Mix

Makes 1⅓ cups

A relaxing warm drink after a long day, this coffee is fragrant with cinnamon and orange. Present this mix packed in a vacuum canister with a porcelain coffeepot and matching coffee cups, all assembled in a basket. Include a package of Molasses Cookie Mix (see page 93), too.

⅓ cup instant coffee
  (decaffeinated or
  regular)
½ cup cocoa powder
½ cup nonfat dry milk

1 teaspoon ground
  cinnamon
2 teaspoons dried orange
  peel

Combine the ingredients in a small bowl. Stir until the mixture is blended. Store in an airtight container.

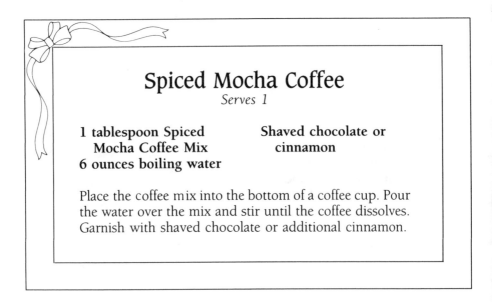

Spiced Mocha Coffee
Serves 1

1 tablespoon Spiced
  Mocha Coffee Mix
6 ounces boiling water

Shaved chocolate or
  cinnamon

Place the coffee mix into the bottom of a coffee cup. Pour the water over the mix and stir until the coffee dissolves. Garnish with shaved chocolate or additional cinnamon.

Hot Chocolate Mix

Makes 4¼ cups

O ne is never too old to enjoy hot chocolate, and this is a special way to share it with a friend. Pack it into a basket with Snickerdoodle Mix (see page 96), candy canes, marshmallows, and some pretty mugs. Or, pack half-cup portions into cellophane bags, place the bag in the mug, and tie it with ribbons.

3 cups powdered milk	**½ cup cocoa**
¾ cup sugar	**Dash of salt**

Sift the ingredients into a large bowl. Pack the mix into airtight containers.

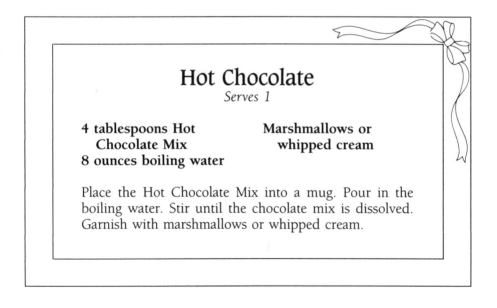

Hot Chocolate
Serves 1

4 tablespoons Hot Chocolate Mix	**Marshmallows or whipped cream**
8 ounces boiling water	

Place the Hot Chocolate Mix into a mug. Pour in the boiling water. Stir until the chocolate mix is dissolved. Garnish with marshmallows or whipped cream.

Minted Citrus Tea Mix

Makes 1¼ cups

T his blend is delicious cold or hot. Pack Minted Citrus Tea Mix
into a glass canister and arrange it in a basket with a tea strainer,
two covered teacups, party (colored) sugar, and a package of Oatmeal
Cookie Mix (see page 95). During the summer, this makes a lovely gift
basket with a pitcher, four iced-tea glasses, iced-tea spoons, several
fresh lemons, and a mint plant.

½ pound orange Pekoe
tea
2 tablespoons dried mint
leaves

2 tablespoons whole
cloves
1 tablespoon dried lemon
peel

Combine the ingredients in a medium bowl. Stir to blend. Pack the tea
into an airtight canister or container.

Minted Citrus Tea

Serves 1

**1 teaspoon Minted
Citrus Tea Mix**

6 ounces boiling water

Fill a tea strainer with the Minted Citrus Tea Mix. Lay the strainer in the bottom of a teacup. Add the boiling water. Allow to steep for 5 minutes.

Minted Citrus Sun Tea

Makes 1 quart

**¼ cup Minted Citrus
Tea Mix**

1 quart water

Place the Minted Citrus Tea Mix in the bottom of a glass pitcher. Add water and cover the pitcher. Allow the pitcher to sit in direct sunlight for 4 to 6 hours. Strain the tea leaves, and refrigerate the tea.

Spiced Tea Mix

Makes 1¾ cups

S cented with citrus, cinnamon, and cloves, this brew is a delightful change of pace for coffee and tea drinkers alike. Pack Spiced Tea Mix in a cellophane bag and then place it on a tray with a teapot and two teacups with saucers.

1 tablespoon dried lemon
  peel
2 teaspoons whole cloves
4 cinnamon sticks,
  crushed

2 tablespoons loose tea
  leaves
1 tablespoon dried orange
  peel
1½ cups sugar

Combine all the ingredients in a bowl. Place the mixture in a cheese-cloth bag, and store in an airtight container.

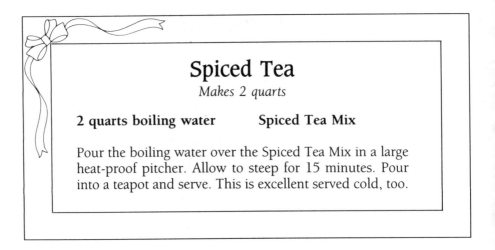

Spiced Tea

Makes 2 quarts

2 quarts boiling water   Spiced Tea Mix

Pour the boiling water over the Spiced Tea Mix in a large heat-proof pitcher. Allow to steep for 15 minutes. Pour into a teapot and serve. This is excellent served cold, too.

Mulled Cider Mix

Makes ¼ cup

Mulled Cider Mix makes the perfect autumn hostess gift when given in a basket with Molasses Cookie Mix (see page 93) or Irish Soda Bread Mix (see page 70), along with a heat-proof pitcher and a quart of apple cider. Tuck in a pint bottle of rum or brandy to spice up the cider.

1 teaspoon whole allspice　　**6 whole cloves**
2 sticks cinnamon　　　　　　**⅛ teaspoon ginger**

Place all the ingredients into a cheesecloth packet.

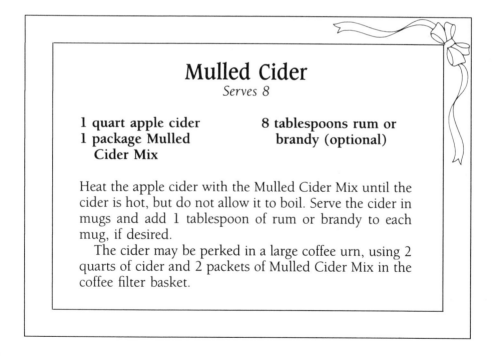

Mulled Cider

Serves 8

1 quart apple cider　　　　**8 tablespoons rum or**
1 package Mulled　　　　　　**brandy (optional)**
Cider Mix

Heat the apple cider with the Mulled Cider Mix until the cider is hot, but do not allow it to boil. Serve the cider in mugs and add 1 tablespoon of rum or brandy to each mug, if desired.

The cider may be perked in a large coffee urn, using 2 quarts of cider and 2 packets of Mulled Cider Mix in the coffee filter basket.

Warm Spiced Cranberry Cider Mix

Makes ⅔ cup

T his spicy cider tastes delicious after winter sports, so here's just the gift for a hostess on a ski vacation. Pack this mix in a zip-type bag and store it in a heat-proof crock, decorated with streamer ribbons. If you'd like to give a whimsical hostess gift, tie the bag to the neck of a stuffed Saint Bernard.

½ cup dried cranberries
12 cinnamon sticks
½ teaspoon crushed
  whole cloves

2 tablespoons whole
  allspice

In a small bowl, stir the cranberries and spices together. Store the ingredients in an airtight container.

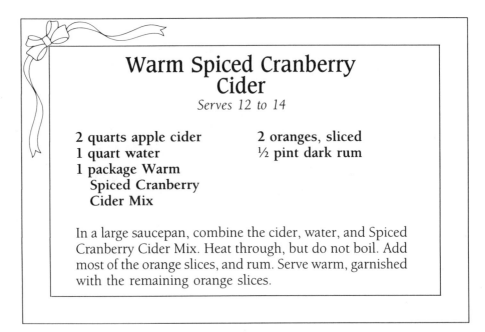

Warm Spiced Cranberry Cider

Serves 12 to 14

2 quarts apple cider
1 quart water
1 package Warm
  Spiced Cranberry
  Cider Mix

2 oranges, sliced
½ pint dark rum

In a large saucepan, combine the cider, water, and Spiced Cranberry Cider Mix. Heat through, but do not boil. Add most of the orange slices, and rum. Serve warm, garnished with the remaining orange slices.

Hot Buttered Rum Mix

Makes 6 cups

Hot Buttered Rum Mix makes a sweet housewarming gift or offering to a host on a cold, snowy night. Pack the mix in a decorative crock, then place it in a basket with a bottle of dark rum, four mugs, whole nutmeg, and a small nutmeg grater.

1 pound butter	½ teaspoon ground
2 pounds brown sugar	nutmeg
1½ tablespoons cinnamon	1 teaspoon vanilla extract

In a large bowl, soften the butter and gradually cream in the remaining ingredients. Refrigerate or freeze.

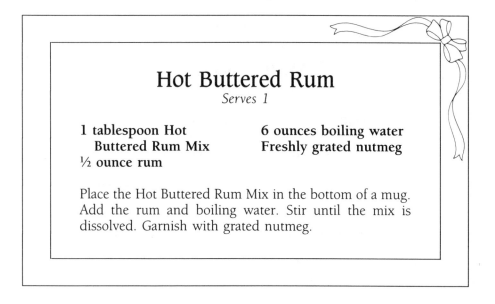

Hot Buttered Rum
Serves 1

1 tablespoon Hot	6 ounces boiling water
Buttered Rum Mix	Freshly grated nutmeg
½ ounce rum	

Place the Hot Buttered Rum Mix in the bottom of a mug. Add the rum and boiling water. Stir until the mix is dissolved. Garnish with grated nutmeg.

Mulled Wine Spice Mix

Makes ¾ cup

A nother winner on a cold night. Give this mix in a basket with a set of mugs, coasters, a bottle of dry red wine, and some oranges.

10 sticks cinnamon, broken into pieces
⅓ cup whole cloves
⅓ cup whole allspice

½ teaspoon ground nutmeg
2 tablespoons dried orange peel

Combine all the ingredients in a bowl. Store the mix in an airtight container.

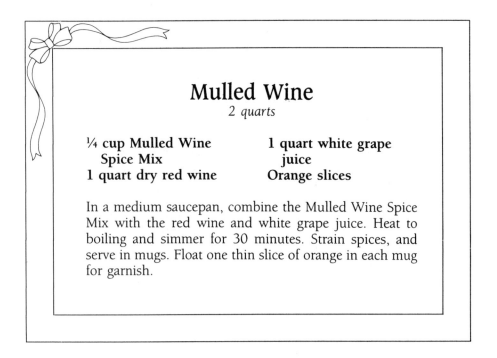

Mulled Wine

2 quarts

¼ cup Mulled Wine Spice Mix
1 quart dry red wine

1 quart white grape juice
Orange slices

In a medium saucepan, combine the Mulled Wine Spice Mix with the red wine and white grape juice. Heat to boiling and simmer for 30 minutes. Strain spices, and serve in mugs. Float one thin slice of orange in each mug for garnish.

Hot Spiced Wine Mix

Makes 1½ cups

A wintry night, a roaring fireplace, and this gift make an inviting trio. Fragrant with spices, Hot Spiced Wine Mix can be packed in a basket with a bottle of dry red wine, a thermos, and some mugs.

1½ cups sugar
1½ teaspoons ground cinnamon

½ teaspoon ground cloves
½ teaspoon ground allspice

Combine all the ingredients and store in an airtight container.

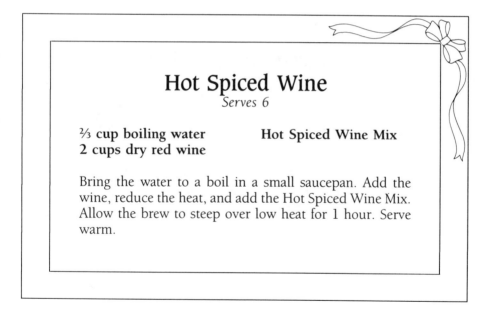

Hot Spiced Wine
Serves 6

⅔ cup boiling water
2 cups dry red wine

Hot Spiced Wine Mix

Bring the water to a boil in a small saucepan. Add the wine, reduce the heat, and add the Hot Spiced Wine Mix. Allow the brew to steep over low heat for 1 hour. Serve warm.

Spiced Cherry Wine Mix

Makes 1½ cups

D ried cherries give this warm wine an unusual flavor. Pack the mix in a basket along with two bottles of dry red wine, several fresh lemons, a box of crackers, and some imported cheeses.

½ cup dried cherries
1 cup sugar

4 sticks cinnamon
12 whole cloves

Combine the ingredients in a bowl and store in an airtight container.

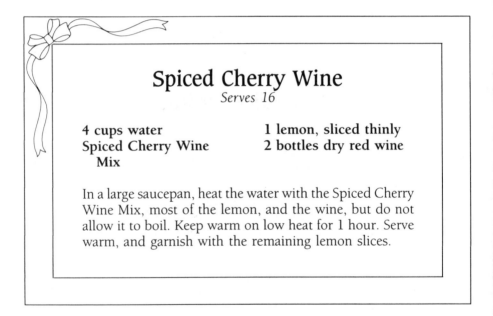

Spiced Cherry Wine

Serves 16

4 cups water
Spiced Cherry Wine
  Mix

1 lemon, sliced thinly
2 bottles dry red wine

In a large saucepan, heat the water with the Spiced Cherry Wine Mix, most of the lemon, and the wine, but do not allow it to boil. Keep warm on low heat for 1 hour. Serve warm, and garnish with the remaining lemon slices.

Fresh Herb Baskets

Fresh herb baskets are a living gift that will keep on giving, either in a kitchen window or transplanted into an herb garden. Line your basket with clear contact paper to prevent leaking, or place a large plastic saucer in the bottom. Lay sphagnum moss (available at most nurseries) in the bottom of the basket and around the sides. Remove the plants from their pots and arrange them in the basket. Cover the dirt with more moss. Water the plants lightly. The plants should be watered only when the top layer of dirt feels dry (about 2 tablespoons per plant).

At certain times of the year you may have trouble finding good-quality fresh herbs. If so, plant them from seeds in your window, or mail order fresh plants from Taylor's Herb Garden in Vista, California (see Source Guide).

To create a festive look for a special birthday or at holiday time, wrap these baskets in colored cellophane and tie them with coordinating ribbons.

Many alternate theme packaging ideas will be found in the pages that follow, inspired by the particular recipes offered.

Shellfish Seasoning Basket

T his basket should contain dill, lemon thyme, French tarragon, and chervil. Line a large ceramic seashell or shell-like container with clear contact paper. Place a layer of moss in the bottom of the basket and around the sides. Plant the herbs over the moss, and cover the top of the dirt with more moss. Water the plants using ¼ to ⅓ cup water.

This basket would be lovely paired with French Baguette Mix (see page 71).

The herbs in this basket will enhance any seafood or shellfish dish. They may be blended with butter to make a seasoned herb butter for grilled shellfish, or used to make the Marinated Shrimp appetizer that follows.

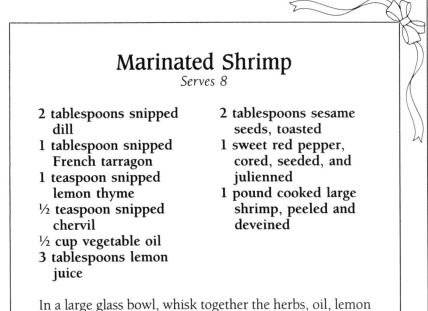

Marinated Shrimp
Serves 8

2 tablespoons snipped
  dill
1 tablespoon snipped
  French tarragon
1 teaspoon snipped
  lemon thyme
½ teaspoon snipped
  chervil
½ cup vegetable oil
3 tablespoons lemon
  juice

2 tablespoons sesame
  seeds, toasted
1 sweet red pepper,
  cored, seeded, and
  julienned
1 pound cooked large
  shrimp, peeled and
  deveined

In a large glass bowl, whisk together the herbs, oil, lemon
juice, and sesame seeds. Add the red pepper and shrimp
and toss the mixture until the shrimp are coated. Refrigerate the shrimp for 2 to 4 hours before serving. Drain and
serve on French bread rounds.

Fish Seasoning Basket

T his basket offers fine seasonings for grilled, poached, or fried fish. To create a marine motif, plant the herbs in a large cork basket decorated with tropical fish napkin rings or small glass fishing floats tied to the handles. Plant French tarragon, chives, chervil, and parsley.

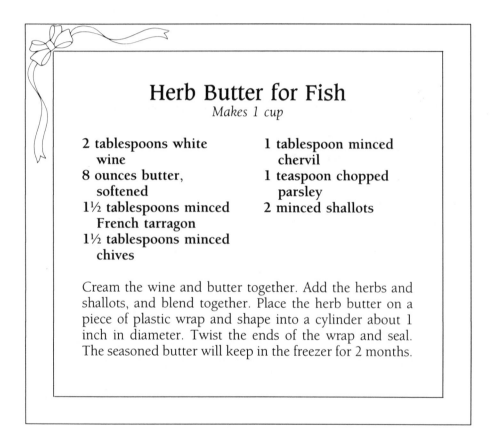

Herb Butter for Fish
Makes 1 cup

2 tablespoons white
  wine
8 ounces butter,
  softened
1½ tablespoons minced
  French tarragon
1½ tablespoons minced
  chives

1 tablespoon minced
  chervil
1 teaspoon chopped
  parsley
2 minced shallots

Cream the wine and butter together. Add the herbs and shallots, and blend together. Place the herb butter on a piece of plastic wrap and shape into a cylinder about 1 inch in diameter. Twist the ends of the wrap and seal. The seasoned butter will keep in the freezer for 2 months.

Fines Herbes Basket

*F*ines herbes is a blend of sweet herbs of French origins. They are especially good in gravies, sauces, fish, and vegetables. A basket of fines herbes can turn an impromptu meal into something of a culinary triumph. These plants could be packed in a country wooden basket lined with a red-and-white checked napkin hanging over the sides and protected with a plastic saucer in the bottom. Include one plant each of French tarragon, chives, parsley, and chervil. Tie a little French whisk to the basket handle for a final Gallic touch.

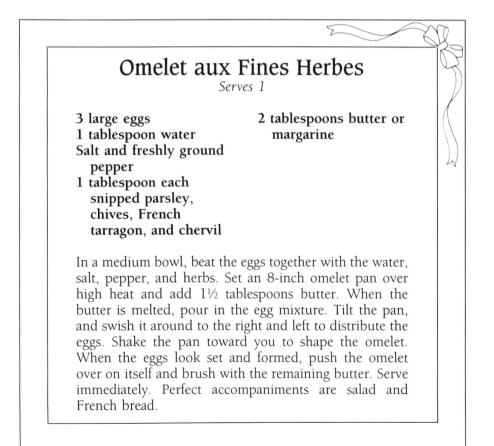

Omelet aux Fines Herbes
Serves 1

3 large eggs
1 tablespoon water
Salt and freshly ground
  pepper
1 tablespoon each
  snipped parsley,
  chives, French
  tarragon, and chervil

2 tablespoons butter or
  margarine

In a medium bowl, beat the eggs together with the water, salt, pepper, and herbs. Set an 8-inch omelet pan over high heat and add 1½ tablespoons butter. When the butter is melted, pour in the egg mixture. Tilt the pan, and swish it around to the right and left to distribute the eggs. Shake the pan toward you to shape the omelet. When the eggs look set and formed, push the omelet over on itself and brush with the remaining butter. Serve immediately. Perfect accompaniments are salad and French bread.

Fines Herbes Sauce Basket

T his creamy sauce is delicious over chicken breasts or vegetables. Line the longest bread basket you can find with bright linen dish towels. Assemble one plant each of French tarragon, chives, parsley, and chervil (each on its own plastic saucer to keep towels dry), and three or four empty sauce jars, about the same height as the plants. Place in the basket, alternating plants and gaily beribboned jars, which can later be filled with Fines Herbes Sauce made by your gift recipient.

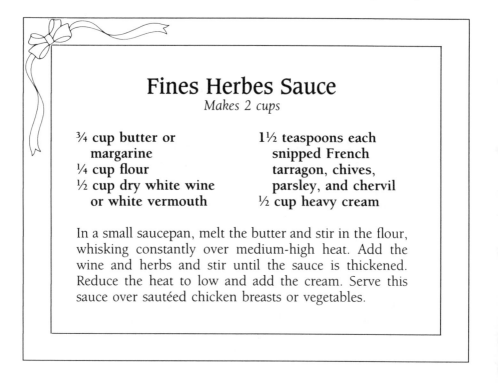

Fines Herbes Sauce
Makes 2 cups

¾ cup butter or
  margarine
¼ cup flour
½ cup dry white wine
  or white vermouth

1½ teaspoons each
  snipped French
  tarragon, chives,
  parsley, and chervil
½ cup heavy cream

In a small saucepan, melt the butter and stir in the flour, whisking constantly over medium-high heat. Add the wine and herbs and stir until the sauce is thickened. Reduce the heat to low and add the cream. Serve this sauce over sautéed chicken breasts or vegetables.

Italian Herb Basket

A combination of traditional Italian herbs, this basket is special when paired with Pizza Dough Mix (see page 88), a bottle of Chianti, extra virgin olive oil, and a small bottle of red wine vinegar. Line a white basket with clear contact paper. Lay moss over the bottom and sides of the basket. Plant one unpotted plant each of basil, oregano, and Italian flat-leaf parsley in the basket. Add additional soil if necessary, and top with more moss, then moisten with ¼ cup water. Plant a small Italian flag in the garden and tie red and green streamer ribbons to the sides of the basket.

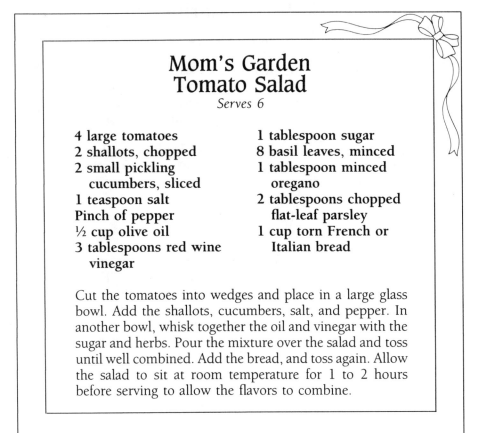

Mom's Garden Tomato Salad
Serves 6

4 large tomatoes
2 shallots, chopped
2 small pickling
　cucumbers, sliced
1 teaspoon salt
Pinch of pepper
½ cup olive oil
3 tablespoons red wine
　vinegar

1 tablespoon sugar
8 basil leaves, minced
1 tablespoon minced
　oregano
2 tablespoons chopped
　flat-leaf parsley
1 cup torn French or
　Italian bread

Cut the tomatoes into wedges and place in a large glass bowl. Add the shallots, cucumbers, salt, and pepper. In another bowl, whisk together the oil and vinegar with the sugar and herbs. Pour the mixture over the salad and toss until well combined. Add the bread, and toss again. Allow the salad to sit at room temperature for 1 to 2 hours before serving to allow the flavors to combine.

Barbecue Herb Basket

H ere's a great summertime barbecue basket, or a thoughtful gift for Father's Day. Group one potted plant each of rosemary, oregano, lemon thyme, and parsley in a small-handled basket. Place this basket into a large split-ash open picnic basket, and include an apron and matching oven mitt, shish kabob skewers, and a chef's hat.

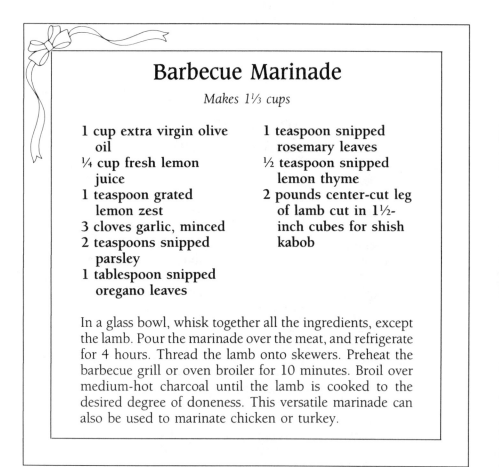

Barbecue Marinade

Makes 1⅓ cups

1 cup extra virgin olive oil

¼ cup fresh lemon juice

1 teaspoon grated lemon zest

3 cloves garlic, minced

2 teaspoons snipped parsley

1 tablespoon snipped oregano leaves

1 teaspoon snipped rosemary leaves

½ teaspoon snipped lemon thyme

2 pounds center-cut leg of lamb cut in 1½-inch cubes for shish kabob

In a glass bowl, whisk together all the ingredients, except the lamb. Pour the marinade over the meat, and refrigerate for 4 hours. Thread the lamb onto skewers. Preheat the barbecue grill or oven broiler for 10 minutes. Broil over medium-hot charcoal until the lamb is cooked to the desired degree of doneness. This versatile marinade can also be used to marinate chicken or turkey.

Garlic Herb Basket

A ny host or hostess would welcome this useful ensemble. Line a round white basket with moss, place a white dip bowl in the center, and surround with potted plants of parsley, chives, thyme, rosemary, garlic chives, and elephant garlic—each on a plastic saucer to catch moisture. Fill the dip bowl with a set of measuring spoons, a garlic press, and a pretty little herb scissors. Be sure to have the plants freshly watered when you deliver the gift basket, which can be wrapped in colored tissue paper twisted into a big pompon on top.

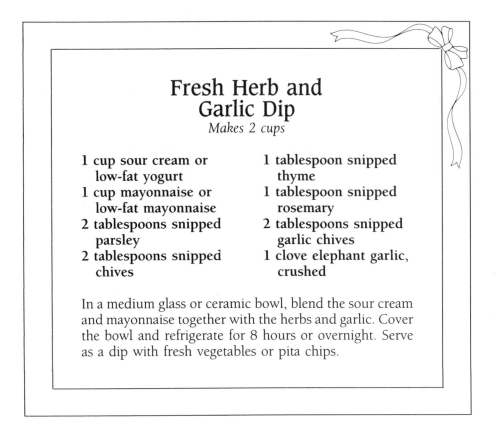

Fresh Herb and Garlic Dip
Makes 2 cups

1 cup sour cream or
  low-fat yogurt
1 cup mayonnaise or
  low-fat mayonnaise
2 tablespoons snipped
  parsley
2 tablespoons snipped
  chives

1 tablespoon snipped
  thyme
1 tablespoon snipped
  rosemary
2 tablespoons snipped
  garlic chives
1 clove elephant garlic,
  crushed

In a medium glass or ceramic bowl, blend the sour cream and mayonnaise together with the herbs and garlic. Cover the bowl and refrigerate for 8 hours or overnight. Serve as a dip with fresh vegetables or pita chips.

Basil Basket

B asil is an aromatic plant that comes in green or purple leaf coloring. This herb adds an unusual and aromatic flavor to many dishes, and can be used in main courses as well as in breads and pasta dishes. The basil garden looks great in a white basket with a handle. Twist green and purple ribbon around the handle and tie the ribbons where the handle meets the basket. Line the basket with clear contact paper, and spread moss along the bottom and sides. Plant two 4-inch pots each of Opal and green basil. Cover the dirt with more moss, and water lightly. You may want to give this basket with some pasta and a French Baguette Mix (see page 71).

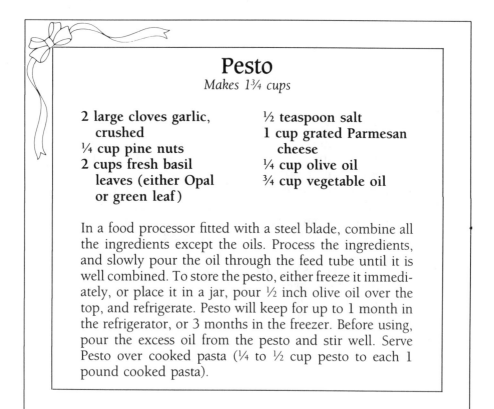

Pesto
Makes 1¾ cups

2 large cloves garlic,
  crushed
¼ cup pine nuts
2 cups fresh basil
  leaves (either Opal
  or green leaf)

½ teaspoon salt
1 cup grated Parmesan
  cheese
¼ cup olive oil
¾ cup vegetable oil

In a food processor fitted with a steel blade, combine all the ingredients except the oils. Process the ingredients, and slowly pour the oil through the feed tube until it is well combined. To store the pesto, either freeze it immediately, or place it in a jar, pour ½ inch olive oil over the top, and refrigerate. Pesto will keep for up to 1 month in the refrigerator, or 3 months in the freezer. Before using, pour the excess oil from the pesto and stir well. Serve Pesto over cooked pasta (¼ to ½ cup pesto to each 1 pound cooked pasta).

Poultry Seasoning Basket

G iven at Thanksgiving or Christmas, this delightful and timely basket offers herbs to enhance the flavors of holiday poultry. Plant one 2-inch pot each of rosemary, sage, summer savory, marjoram, and thyme in a turkey basket or ceramic planter. Or give the plants in their pots, each on its own saucer, placed in a round basket with a bag of fresh cranberries nestled in the center.

Old-Fashioned Turkey Stuffing
Serves 8 to 10

½ cup butter
1 tablespoon each
  snipped rosemary,
  savory, sage,
  marjoram, and thyme
1 large onion, chopped

3 ribs celery, chopped
2½ cups chicken broth
8 cups stale French
  bread cubes

In a large skillet, melt the butter and add the herbs, onion, and celery. Sauté until vegetables are limp, but not browned. Add the chicken broth and bring to a boil. Place the bread cubes in a large bowl, pour the broth mixture over them, and mix well. Stuff turkey with mixture, or bake in a greased, uncovered 3-quart casserole for 1 hour and baste with turkey drippings or additional butter.

Source Guide

Chocolates

Ghirardelli Chocolate Company
1111–139th Avenue
San Leandro, CA 94578-2671
(415) 483-6970

Ghirardelli makes ground chocolate for use in the Ghirardelli Chocolate Cake (see page 105), and also sells cocoa, chocolate chips, and bulk chocolate. Write for their free catalog.

Containers

Crate and Barrel
P.O. Box 3057
Northbrook, IL 60090
(800) 323-5461 (toll-free)

Crate and Barrel stores are located all over the United States, and they have an excellent mail-order catalog offering good buys on glass jars and containers, as well as linens. Call for their free catalog.

Eucalyptus Stoneware
2201 San Dieguito Road
Del Mar, CA 92014
(619) 755-5656

This small, quality company carries ceramic baskets that can go directly into the oven for warming breads, as well as for use in making a fresh-herb basket. Call or write for the retail outlet nearest you, or you can order their long French bread basket from the Williams-Sonoma catalog.

Pier One Imports
301 Commerce Street,
Suite 600
Fort Worth, TX 76161
(800) 447-4371 (toll-free)

Pier One is a chain of stores that carry linens, glass, and woodenware, as well as home furnishings. Their containers are inexpensive and of high quality. Especially lovely are their green Italian glass containers for a variety of mixes.

Williams-Sonoma
Mail Order Department
P.O. Box 7456
San Francisco, CA 94120–7456
(800) 541-2233 (toll-free)
FAX: (415) 421-5153

This is the mail-order division for their beautiful gourmet stores. If you do not live near a Williams-Sonoma store, a tour through their catalog may entice you to visit soon. They carry beautiful containers, as well as chefs' tools, dried fruits, some spices, specialty oils and vinegars, and other fancy food items.

Herbs and Spices

Select Origins Herbs and Spices
Box N
Southampton, NY 11968
(800) 822-2092 (toll-free)
Free catalog
Select Origins sells dried herbs, spices, dried cherries, cranberries, and other fancy foods. Extremely helpful on the phone with any problem, this store will sell in "catering sizes" if you request it. The herbs and spices are of the highest quality and come in functional, small flat jars for easy stacking.

Taylor's Herb Garden
1535 Lone Oak Road
Vista, CA
(619) 727-3485
FAX: (619) 727-0289
Taylor's mail orders fresh herbs all over the world. The staff is helpful over the phone. Send $3.00 for catalog.

Index

smoked salmon pizza, 90
see also Shellfish
Fitz-Patrick's Boston baked beans, 33
Fitz-Patrick's Boston baked beans mix, 33
Focaccia, 87
Focaccia mix, 86
French baguette mix, 71
  companion mixes for, 16, 20, 30, 36, 40, 51, 54, 126, 134
French baguettes, 71
Fresh herb and garlic dip, 133
Fresh herb baskets, *see* Herb baskets
Fresh mozzarella-basil pizza, 90
Frosting, 83
  cream cheese, 105
Fruit(ed):
  curried rice with, 48
  curried rice with, mix, 48
  rice, 42
  rice mix, 42, 49

G

Garlic and fresh herb dip, 133
Garlic herb basket, 133
Ghirardelli chocolate, 104, 136
  cake, 105
  cake mix, 104
Gingerbread:
  cake, 108
  cake mix, 108
  cookie mix, 94
  cookies, 94
Ginger spice muffin mix, 66
Ginger spice muffins, 66
Grilled lemon chicken, 7
Grilled vegetables, 9
Gumbo, New Orleans, 31
Gumbo mix, New Orleans, 30

H

Healthy heart chicken, 11
Herb(s), herbed, 1
  butter for fish, 128

buying in quantity, xii
containers for, x
fresh, and garlic dip, 133
popover mix, 80
popovers, 80
source guide for, 137
see also Seasoning mixes
Herb baskets, 125–135
  barbecue, 50, 132
  basil, 134
  fines herbes, 129
  fines herbes sauce, 130
  fish seasoning, 128
  garlic, 133
  Italian, 131
  poultry seasoning, 135
  shellfish seasoning, 126
Herbes de Provence mix, 16
  ratatouille, 17
Honey:
  nut rice, 47
  nut rice mix, 47
  whole wheat bread, 73
  whole wheat bread mix, 26, 72
Hot buttered rum, 121
Hot buttered rum mix, 121
Hot chocolate, 115
Hot chocolate mix, 104, 115
Hot cross bun mix, 82
Hot cross buns, 83
Hot spiced wine, 123
Hot spiced wine mix, 123

I

Indian squaw bread, 75
Indian squaw bread mix, 74
Irish soda bread, 70
Irish soda bread mix, 70, 119
Italian herb basket, 131

J

Jambalaya, shrimp, 57
Jambalaya, shrimp, mix, 20, 56